Left Populism in Europe

'An outstanding contribution to understand the shortcomings and yet potentials of the left populist experience ... explains what left populism modestly achieved but also points very convincingly to what it has to do in the future to promote the values of equality, social justice and internationalism.'

—Óscar García Agustín, Associate Professor at
Aalborg University, Denmark

'An important, timely appraisal of the European left, one that will inform and inspire activists.'

—Manuel Cortes, General Secretary of the
Transport Salaried Staffs' Association (TSSA)

'It's been a dramatic decade for left-wing political projects in Greece, Spain, and the UK. Through personal experience, a wealth of interviews and analysis, Prentoulis pulls together an assessment which is vital for anyone who wants to understand the post-crash upsurge of radical politics in Europe.'

—Nick Dearden, Director of Global Justice Now

'Rigorously reflecting on the choreography of contemporary left-wing experiments flirting with left populism in crisis-ridden Europe, Prentoulis offers a challenging first assessment of its political advances, limitations and potential for left strategy.'

—Yannis Stavrakakis, Professor at the
Aristotle University of Thessaloniki, Greece

Left Populism
in Europe

Lessons from
Jeremy Corbyn to Podemos

Marina Prentoulis

PLUTO PRESS

First published 2021 by Pluto Press
345 Archway Road, London N6 5AA

www.plutobooks.com

British Library Cataloguing in Publication Data
A catalogue record for this book is available from the British Library

ISBN   978 0 7453 3764 7   Hardback
ISBN   978 0 7453 3763 0   Paperback
ISBN   978 1 7868 0693 2   PDF eBook
ISBN   978 1 7868 0695 6   Kindle eBook
ISBN   978 1 7868 0694 9   EPUB eBook

This book is printed on paper suitable for recycling and made from fully
managed and sustained forest sources. Logging, pulping and manufacturing
processes are expected to conform to the environmental standards of the
country of origin.

Typeset by Stanford DTP Services, Northampton, England

Simultaneously printed in the United Kingdom and United States of America

In memory of my grandmother,
Despina Manoli (1920–2017).

Contents

Acknowledgements

This book was written as left populism started to recede in Europe and Brexit was well underway, so with less political commitments I tried to reflect on the events of the past few years. I draw on interviews I conducted and articles I wrote during this period. Material which didn't make it into this book will hopefully be discussed in future papers. Since the financial crisis of 2008 I have crossed paths with many comrades committed to the fight against austerity in Europe. Each one of them has been a source of inspiration even if the views in this book may not reflect their own.

I am indebted to many people for their continues support, first and foremost to my family, Leonidas, Sofia and Remy Prentoulis and Maria Spanou. My good friend and colleague Lasse Thomassen has always been by my side with his advice and comments on the manuscript. Kevin Conallen made sure that I could always turn to him for encouragement and life wisdom. I would also like to thank Tom Walker for helping with the editing and Michael Klontzas for comments on the Introduction. Last but not least I would like to thank my editor, David Castle, whose patience and advice made this book possible.

Introduction: Why Left Populism?

The term 'populism' is used repeatedly to describe the politics of the last ten years across the world from Spain to Brazil and Venezuela and from Britain to the US. A number of political commentators have used, abused and loathed the term, and the more it is used the more it turns into an easy derogatory term that inhibits further analysis of specific political phenomena. For the mass audience with no specialisation in political theory and populism, the term has become synonymous with 'deception' and 'demagogy' and this perception is what this book aims to challenge. Instead, it proposes the examination of populism as a political logic, a way of doing politics that can be associated with different political actors, on the left and on the right, some visionaries as well as some deceitful demagogues. To put it simply, populism is a way of doing politics and it is the particular content that makes it good or bad.

The context in which the 'populist' hype appeared in the historical period discussed in this book is the global financial crisis of 2007–8 and its aftermath, although the roots of the problem can be traced back to the beginnings of economic globalisation. In focusing on this particular incident what soon became evident was not only an economic crisis but also a deep crisis of political representation. The financial crisis, unexpected by most economists, revealed in a painful way that what was perceived as a functioning if unequal economic system was in effect based on the creation of wealth based on specu- lation and risky practices, which could end the livelihoods of ordinary people in the wink of an eye. The queues outside Northern Rock bank when it collapsed in 2007, the employees of Lehman Brothers leaving the building carrying their personal possessions in boxes, became the shocking visualisation of the fall of powerful institutions which had given in to a risk economy. The unprecedented crowds occupying the squares of Greece and Spain in 2011 became the image of what a crisis of political representation looks like: people who had never before demonstrated, from different backgrounds, all came together to demand the reform of a political system (with national and international institutions) that instead of protecting during dire times took the route of severe austerity measures, inflicting even more pain on the people that it was supposed to represent.

In the political arena, new parties and leaders emerged from both the left and the right, asserting that they would represent these people. They were very different from the centrist technocratic parties and leaders that up to that point were dominating the political scene. Yes, they did aim to represent 'the people' but not by finding a 'moderate', lukewarm position somewhere in the centre of the political spectrum, a position that for decades now had aligned itself with the neoliberal paradigm no matter if we speak of centre-left or centre-right parties. The newcomers were against the political and economic mainstream, they were themselves 'outsiders', either of the 'radical left' or on the 'far right'. Neither of the two, although coming from very different world perspectives, minced their words; neither seemed to care much about the 'etiquette' of the political game. Even more than that, they seemed to want to overturn the gameboard altogether. The leaders of these parties, Alexis Tsipras (Greece), Pablo Iglesias (Spain), Marine Le Pen (France), Jeremy Corbyn (UK) and others were charismatic and they seemed to connect with 'the people' in a direct way that we hadn't seen for some time. Their personal style and their way of communicating were not the only things that differentiated them from the technocrats that proceeded them: they criticised the 'elites' that were responsible for the economic and political mess (national and international) and they seemed to appeal across economic and social strata, dividing the political space into 'us' and 'them'. Most Western liberal democracies of the type I am discussing here, however, operate on the assumption of consensus. In effect that has come to mean that diverse political views can coexist in a relatively pluralistic environment without generating strong negative emotions, and that emerging grievances and demands are addressed (successfully or unsuccessfully) within the existing political system without challenging the political system as a whole. This is not the case when society is divided to 'us' and 'them', a division that in effect questions the peaceful coexistence of both poles.

This polarisation of society sends chills down the spine of the political establishment exactly because it challenges the ability of existing institutions to accommodate both poles without significant reform. It is not surprising then that journalists and commentators (themselves instrumental in the creation of consensus) embark on a crusade to condemn the 'populists' and their politics, usually without really engaging with the grievances that the populists were addressing. From there on, every phenomenon that is despised by the mainstream is labelled as 'populist', creating the populist hype. The only thing unusual about the cases I examine was that populism was emerging in Europe and the US, environments that had embraced the liberal democratic consensus and neoliberalism as the only alternative, rather than in societies marked by sharper divisions (like in Latin America). Furthermore, for a long time the bureaucratisation of the political field seemed to be keeping 'the people' out of politics. Yes, there were movements, protests and grievances before, but not on the same scale nor with such a dangerously unruly desire for a different political paradigm. By contrast Latin America seemed to have more stories to tell about populism and populist leaders, from Juan Perón (president of Argentina, 1946–55) to Hugo Chávez (president of Venezuela, 1999–2013). A possible explanation is that because of the exclusion and oppression of large groups of citizens from the political process in their respective countries, the bringing together of 'a people' under the direction of a strong, charismatic leader demanding that the voice of 'the people' is heard was the most successful way to unite and fight against the common enemy, from corrupt national elites to American imperialism. This is why left populism, at least in the past, borrowed heavily from the example of Latin American cases. More recently, the example of Jair Bolsonaro (president of Brazil since 2019) as well as that of Donald Trump (president of the US, 2016–2020) are becoming focal points for understanding contemporary right-wing populism, which although beyond the scope of this book I will return to in a bit.

Western liberal democracies had been convinced for decades that their institutions offered checks and balances for a functioning democracy, and that these institutions were the best and possibly the only ones capable of bringing change if needed. Over the last few decades these institutions have been run by technocrats and experts who claimed to know better what 'the people' needed as long as the latter legitimised them by voting every few years. This was called by some scholars the post-democratic condition: a type of democracy that didn't really need the 'demos' to engage and where politics is the business of those who knew better and had 'expertise'.

Populism (of either the right or the left) came to challenge the bureaucratisation of democracy after the financial crisis and although it did not always lead to victory, today we can reflect on what it did achieve, what it didn't and where it went wrong for the progressive left actors. The concept of populism is useful, however, because it describes something beyond the cases I mention above: it describes a way of doing politics, a political logic. We may want to believe there are many different ways of doing politics, but if we look at the logic behind them rather than the particular content they can be reduced to two broad methods: either by accepting the existing institutions (of any period and context) and bureaucratically trying to implement gradual change without needing 'a people' to take a stand; or via a populist logic which divides the political space into two camps and challenges the establishment (electorally or in the streets, peacefully or not). This book aims to look beyond the particularity of the cases it explores from the last ten years to draw some general principles, but at the same time any analysis of a political movement has to be grounded in a reading of its context in order to reflect on the different strategic choices of populism.

The Populist Far Right and the Populist Radical Left

From the financial crisis until the end of 2020 the populist far right emerged as the main electoral winner in Europe and beyond. In the US Trump won the 2016 election by verbally assaulting not only his opponent, Hillary Clinton, but also women who accused him of sexual misconduct and the media which, he claimed, conspired against him.[1] His almost direct endorsements of white supremacists and his obsession with theatricality rather than substance drove the definition of 'populism' for mainstream media, and not surprisingly some scholars ready to analyse populism as well as the majority of the media started to define populism as a threat to democracy. Although this may feel plausible for politicians like Nigel Farage, Donald Trump or Boris Johnson, this is the case for the particular populist, authoritarian far right. It is true that populism seems at odds with the pluralism of liberal democracy by putting 'the will of the people' above

4

all, and ultimately through the danger of having the will of the people collapsing into the will of the leader or the party.[2] This book, however, explores different forms of populism. It views left populism as a serious attempt to find what is in the best interests of the majority, the 99 per cent. In this perspective populism not only evokes 'the people' but it recognises the difference of opinions within this body. It goes further than just registering them, as is often the case in liberal democracy, by giving them space and creating the forums for disagreement which ultimately aim to be productive and channelled in an egalitarian and emancipatory direction.

A final point on the populist far right (even if the analysis of the right is beyond the scope of this book). One of the political developments regarding the far right is that in some cases (those less chilling than Trump's for example) it has been legitimised and incorporated within the previously 'respectable' right. This is the case in Greece where the collapse of Golden Dawn (a Nazi, racist and nationalistic party) is down to the trial of a number of their MPs for the murder of migrants, trade unionists and antifascist singer Pavlos Fyssas. Although in the 2019 general election Golden Dawn did not enter parliament, unable to reach the benchmark 3 per cent of the vote, the anti-migrant sentiment has been mainstreamed by the governing right-wing New Democracy party. The latter is also staffed by far-right ex-comrades of some of the Golden Dawn leaders.

In Britain, despite the collapse of the UK Independence Party (UKIP) vote in 2017, the nationalist and racist rhetoric of their constituency can now find expression in Boris Johnson's comments about Muslim women wearing burkas looking like 'letter boxes', as well as the orchestrated attempt by his government to create panic over migration in order to implement hostile legislation.[3]

While the populist far right is doing well in electoral terms, the results are mixed when left-populist parties come to power. The most successful story seems to be that of Spain where Unidas Podemos[4] have had a coalition agreement with PSOE (the Spanish social democratic party), the first for 80 years, since January 2020. Unidas Podemos support the PSOE-led government in return for a shared government platform, the vice-presidency and four ministers. As in all cases where we have either a left-leaning pretender or an actual left-leaning government the mainstream Spanish media had a feast, accusing Prime Minister Pedro Sánchez of ruling with 'communists' and 'terrorists'. The case of Unidas Podemos is interesting because the outspoken left-populist Íñigo Errejón had already removed himself from the Podemos coalition party and the leader and arch-rival Pablo Iglesias formed Unidas Podemos with the United Left (Izquierda Unida (IU), a more traditional left party than Podemos). It thus shows what happens when a centre-left party (PSOE) is pulled to the left by a party that even without Errejón was from the start articulating 'a people' against austerity and the establishment. Since then the pandemic has put the Spanish government under a lot of stress, but a number of positive steps early on, like the 200 billion euro package at the start of the pandemic for supporting businesses and workers,[5] have so far sustained public support.[6] The opposition right-wing People's Party (PP) has accused the government for poor management of the pandemic and the far-right Vox has accused the government of trying to replace democracy with a totalitarian state. While the pandemic unfolds, it is difficult to predict where the coalition government will land after the devastating fatalities of the pandemic.

Syriza in Greece also had electoral success. After forming a government in 2015 and staying in power for four years, it lost the 2019 national election to the right-wing New Democracy party and is currently the main opposition party. Electorally, Syriza has seen the biggest success of the parties of the left exhibiting populist elements but its popularity declined when it had to implement the memorandum agreement between Troika (European Commission, European Central Bank (ECB) and the International Monetary Fund (IMF)) after painful negotiations in the summer of 2015. The Greek people voted Syriza into office a second time after the signing of the memorandum, but from there on the freedom to implement their own policies was significantly diminished. It is, however, the most fascinating case, not only because it was the first party of the left to win national elections after the crisis, but also because it forces us to examine their strategy within very restrictive economic conditions.

The British Labour Party is not a newcomer on the political scene. Under Tony Blair it won elections by aligning itself with neoliberalism and using very successful professional communicators to create a popular, non-threatening image of the party rather than organically engaging with the demands of the people. At that point such an approach was enough when enacted by one of the two main parties in a political system that is designed to exclude newcomers. When Jeremy Corbyn was elected leader of the party in 2015 not only did it move the party to the left but it also gave voice to 'a people', within and outside the party, that wanted to stand up to the party elites and the political establishment as we know it.

The three cases are quite different in many respects, from their respective electoral successes and failures to their policies and mutations. Therefore they offer good comparative ground for left populism and the dynamics of the concept. Each chapter that follows addresses a different moment in the history of these parties. As events started to unfold after the crisis (from 2009 to 2019) I started interviewing activists, party officials and left-wing journalists as well as collecting and analysing documents associated with the anti-austerity movements and parties. Some of these interviews were semi-structured, with clearly defined topics and informed (explicitly or implicitly) systematic research projects which have since been published.[7] Other semi-structured interviews are used here for the first time and direct quotes are given as examples of how some officials and journalists involved in Syriza, Podemos and Labour viewed the trajectory of these parties between 2011 and 2019.[8] I have not tried to exhaust the position of different factions within these parties but rather to consult with those whose perspective according to my assessment could contribute to the discussion on left populism.

Chapter 1 looks at populism as a political logic bringing into being 'a people' that it posits against the corrupt elites, thus dividing the political terrain. Although there are many theorisations of populism I focus on the work of Ernesto Laclau and Chantal Mouffe and try to tease out the relevance of their disagreement with other theorists. Part of this discussion is the examination of the concept of 'the people', the claims put forward by political leaders and the characteristics of left populism in particular.

Chapter 2 looks at the aftermath of the financial crisis and the movements that emerged at that point, examining how grassroots activity (some instances more than others) enables the creation of 'a people' by bringing diverse demands together.

Chapter 3 looks at the displacement of the demands of the movements (especially around issues of political representation) into the site of electoral politics and parties. By becoming vehicles for the demands of the anti-austerity movements, Syriza, Podemos and the Labour Party had to create, or transform already existing, party structures that enable more horizontal participation. Each party approached the issue differently and although none can claim radically different structures from the traditional parties, they still contributed to the democratisation efforts of the period.

Chapter 4 examines the electoral potential of the three parties by contextualising the decline of social democratic parties during the crisis which created the conditions for the emergence of left-populist parties (Syriza and Podemos). It then moves on to discuss different electoral strategies and electoral campaigns.

Chapter 5 looks at attempts by populist parties to develop left/socialist policies, starting with a historical account of socialist demands. Although all three parties set out to stop austerity policies and change what at that point was still the neoliberal orthodoxy of dealing with crises, they faced different impediments in attempting to implement their agendas. The chapter finishes with a discussion of municipalism as the terrain where more radical programmes can be tried out.

Finally, Chapter 6 examines the role of nationalism and sovereignty in shaping left responses to the negotiations between the Syriza government and the Troika as well as Brexit. When institutions of international cooperation like the EU have themselves been dominated by national interests and neoliberal politics, one has to wonder if there is a possibility of a pan-European populist strategy that will stand up to European elites. The example of the Democracy in Europe Movement 2025 (DiEM25) points towards a type of solidarity and cooperation beyond nation states, and even if it did not bring about any concrete change it does invite us to think of transnationalism.

This book recognises that although in the three cases under examination left populism didn't bring about the change it promised, its potential as a reform strategy has not been exhausted. For its success, however, it will have to take more seriously the role of 'the people' in shaping the organisation, the agenda and the institutions of left-populist parties and governments.

1

The Politics of Left Populism
after the Global Financial Crisis

Left-populist parties started to make gains in Europe following the financial crisis of 2008 and the rise of the Indignados movements in Greece and Spain in 2011. The recession that followed the financial crisis led to the widespread adoption of strict austerity measures which sparked protests across the Southern European countries most badly affected. It is within this context that Podemos was formed in Spain in 2014, electing five members to the European Parliament that same year and becoming the third largest party at the national election the year after. Syriza, a small left coalition, became the main opposition party in Greece at the June 2012 national election and won the January 2015 election. Finally, the Labour Party's membership surge during the 2015 leadership contest gave the previously marginalised left-winger Jeremy Corbyn a landslide victory.

For some this brought to mind the pink tide in Latin America a decade earlier. Behind the latter lay the imposition of policies designed to bring fiscal balance and international competitiveness to indebted countries and imposed by bodies like the IMF and the US Agency for International Development. These policies included privatisation of public services and companies and cuts to social spending. The rejection of these policies and the rise to power of left-wing governments in South America at the dawn of the millennium promised a different future, through distributive policies and an anti-imperialist message. The wave started with the election of Hugo Chávez in Venezuela in 1998. The process accelerated as the world witnessed the collapse of the Argentinian economy and the extensive protests in the country in 2001 leading to the election of Néstor Kirchner in 2003, and with the election of Luiz Inácio Lula da Silva as president of Brazil in the same year, then to Bolivia in 2006 with Evo Morales and to Ecuador in 2007 with Rafael Correa.

These scenes in Argentina were to be repeated ten years later in Greece, as it became clear that the financial crisis of 2008 was to hit Southern Europe hardest: the fear that Greece would default on its huge debt (like Argentina had previously) led to long queues outside Greek banks and people concealing stashes of millions of euros – in tax havens for the wealthy, and under mattresses for those of more modest means.

The big lenders moved into Greece – the IMF, ECB and European Commission known as the Troika – imposing a remedy of the same poison: more neoliberalism, more austerity, more suffering.

In 2011 the people of Greece but also Spain (actually a few days earlier than in Greece) took to the streets, indignant, scared and determined to demand a different future. In Syntagma Square in Athens a huge banner was unveiled with an image of a yellow helicopter – a reference to Argentinian President Fernando de la Rúa fleeing the country by helicopter in 2001. From that moment the Greeks and Spanish were perceived to be the new protagonists of a European 'pink tide' – one that has not yet achieved the same scale of reform as the South American one, but is nevertheless clear in its demand for an alternative to neoliberalism. These new left populists – or as the right-wing populist media across Europe called them, the new 'Chavistas' – were perceived as a threat to the European status quo.

Why 'left populists'? They were populists because as activists, as politicians and as parties they aimed to speak in the name of 'the people'. And left because they were convinced that the mantra of TINA (which claims that 'there is no alternative' to neoliberalism) had to change.

We should, however, examine the concept of left populism more closely in order to dispel some of the misconceptions perpetuated by scholars and commentators alike. Left populism emerges in particular historical moments when the 'establishment' has lost the trust of the people. While the term 'populism' might bring to mind right-wing politicians, left populism hardly bares any resemblance to this when it comes to its programme and vision.

The Question of Representation

The 2008 crisis revealed the faults of the neoliberal economic system, which had permitted a few people to become obscenely wealthy through risk taking and speculation, while producing nothing tangible. This gang of financiers had never pledged their allegiance to democracy, nor to the good of the people of the countries affected. Elected politicians, however, could not escape accountability that easily, and so what started as a financial crisis rapidly became a crisis of political representation.

Representation is not a straightforward concept in political theory. In its everyday use it is understood as reflecting a reality (as in 'representation' in media) but also sometimes as one thing standing in for something else. To take an example from the 2019 UK general election campaign, when Prime Minister Boris Johnson refused to take part in a TV debate on climate change his seat on the Channel 4 programme was occupied by a block of melting ice. This was obviously a joke, but still the block of ice was 'representing', standing for, Johnson's position on climate change, silent while a catastrophe was taking place.

In politics the operation of representation is far from innocent and open to confusion. Think of the media representation of women, for example. When feminist theorists were analysing women's magazines in the 1960s and 1970s they found that women were represented in stereotypical terms, for example as being interested only in domestic life. This was a 'misrepresentation' of women, reducing them to roles assisting a system of domination set up by men.[1] This type of representation rests on how well something is described, which in the example I gave is a distorted, inaccurate or partial representation. (I am sure some people would argue the same about the block of ice incident.)

Politicians can also misrepresent, distort or manipulate the desires of the people they are supposed to represent. Political representation, however, involves an action: doing something for those one represents implies pursuing the interests of those represented. It implies on the one hand authority (citizens must give their consent to those who represent them), while on the other hand it implies that those who have consented can hold the representatives accountable for their actions.[2]

The crisis of representation after the financial crisis stems from these two dimensions of political representation. First, the consent people had given to their elected representatives broke down as news spread of the scale of financial speculation and how badly it had imperilled the global economy. Second, by protesting in the streets and showing the scale of their indignation, as people did in Greece and Spain in

2011, they were holding their political representatives accountable for not pursuing the interests of those they represented.

Here we can turn to Ernesto Laclau's theory of populism to further examine the relationship between representative and represented. When we talk about representation we do not only talk about the process of institutional representation, such as in parliament, but also about other political actors, such as a social movement that 'represents' the people, or a part of it – later on in this chapter I discuss what we mean by 'the people' and how it comes to being as an entity. There is also a more performative dimension here: when a movement, for example, says that it represents the people, or 'speaks for the people', it brings 'the people' into being by doing so. The movement creates the object it represents.

At this point I usually refer to the example of Lenin (think of another leader if you prefer) addressing the people with the phrase: 'You, the working class ... '. Isn't he at that point creating this entity, the 'working class'? This does not mean that the people in front of him didn't exist before he said it, nor that the working class wouldn't exist if he hadn't said it. But by saying it, the people – here, the working class – come into being as a political subject that will act in this historical moment. The working class as a political actor is a point of contention between traditional Marxists and neo- or post-Marxists, so let me stress here that the relationship of representation I am describing is not one-directional. Lenin could have claimed whatever he wanted, but if his claim wasn't taken up by the people he addressed – if the people didn't understand themselves as 'the working class' – he wouldn't be representing much. Representation, then, is a multidimensional process: from the represented to the representative and vice versa.[3]

The reason populist leaders can in some cases claim convincingly that they represent 'the people' is that the people themselves have accepted their claim. After all, anyone can claim that they represent someone. It becomes believable only when the subject to be represented says 'yes, this person represents me'. Only then does any leader's attempt at representing the people gain actual political power. The claims that populism is nothing more than manipulation by a leader are therefore a bit simplistic. There must be the conditions, the demands and the desire of the people in order for a leader to convincingly claim they represent 'the people'. As with any democratic process it is not only about an imposition from the top – thus, populist representation is less top down than assumed. If the claim is *not* embraced by the people, then we have a failed populist project, which may be interesting for academics but has very limited political consequences.

Does populism require a leader, then? Among those interested in populism, some seem more interested in starting not with a leader or a party at election time, but with grassroots activity and movements expressing demands against the establishment. Some call this 'grassroots populism'[4] and see in populism a radical, democratic, left-wing potential. But often a leader becomes the face and voice of a populist project, and for this reason their personality and speeches for example are of interest. They are bringing the populist project to life, so to speak.

Populism and representation are seen in a negative light for some contemporary theorists such as Jan-Werner Müller. He claims that 'the people' according to populists are a 'homogeneous' entity – a claim that, if true, would make populists blind to the diversity of demands and identities involved in a populist project. But the populist theorists (and political actors) we are discussing here have not made such a claim. Despite Müller's attempt to discredit them, they would argue against him, stressing the complexity and differentiation among 'the people', which can make the formation of this kind of collectivity a difficult process.[5]

Müller's assumption is that populism, as a top-down political project, is not serious in understanding and enabling the participation of the people. This may be the case for right-wing populists (although as I said earlier the people have to accept to be represented by these populists) but not for many left-populist projects.

No one can deny however that populism is a controversial label. The issue of populist representation becomes more complex if we look at it as a metaphorical rather than 'real' entity. Theorists and journalists with either a left- or a right-wing agenda often use the term 'populist' as something that is less than 'real' and is more in keeping with the symbolic – in extreme cases, merely a synonym for manipulation. Müller, for example, juxtaposes democratic representation (which liberal democratic institutions offer, according to him) and *symbolic* representation (what populists rely on).[6] He insists that because populists rely on this symbolic type of representation the populist people are not real, and the populist leaders do not really want them to participate continuously in the political community that the leader claims to represent.[7] In his view the populist people is a passive and manipulated people.

The question that persists is: who are 'the people'? The concept of 'the people' is less closely examined and questioned, though it is often defined according to concepts such as national identity. However, isn't this another imaginary construction? The 'nation' is more or less a eighteenth-century invention, albeit one with very real consequences such as the wars waged in the name of one or other national interest. In populism (though there are differences between right-wing and left-wing discourses) 'the people' is often constructed around the idea of a nation. Equally important is who is excluded, who is *not* part of this nation, and this changes according to place, time and circumstances. The 'enemy' of the nation can be the corrupt elites, a foreign power, immigrants and refugees or all of the above.

Let us look closer at how 'the people' come into being. At the beginning there are diverse demands which progressively start to have the same target and become represented by the same party or leader. In this respect these diverse demands start to come together, forming what we could metaphorically call a chain, a chain that unites them in a common struggle. This is how diverse groups of people with different grievances, potentially from different classes, come together to create 'a people'. Are these 'people' a homogeneous entity, as Müller and other theorists have argued? Not really, and this is why I said they formed a chain rather than an undifferentiated mass. Grievances and demands come together in a situation where previous affiliations have broken down and now they are looking for a new name to represent them – to represent the chain as a whole. This name not only represents but constitutes the new entity. On the one hand, this name will represent each link of the chain. On the other hand, it will simultaneously act as the point of identification for each of the links.[8] To give an example: the name representing the different grievances in 2011 in Greece and Spain was 'Indignados'. The name allowed all of the different demands to connect under this umbrella at the same time, by having a name the Indignados came into being.

This process is the double movement of representation I described earlier: something else (here a name) represents the object, but at the same time the object has to identify with the name too. Though it is not necessarily a person, this *name* acts as a label that brings the struggle together (all links of the chain are united under the same umbrella), but at the same time one can still identify the different links.

Class can be one of the links in the chain. Working-class people and their demands (labour demands, economic demands) can be part of this chain – and possibly play a leading role by standing for the chain as a whole, as in the example of Lenin. We have to accept, however, that in the process of different elements coming together to form new identities class holds no necessarily privileged position. It is this statement that brings traditional Marxists and post-Marxists into conflict.

The Question of Class

The role of class in populist theory is a matter of extensive debate, especially on the left. Does populism have a place for class? Or, if we want to stretch it further, can populism be revolutionary in the traditional sense?

I am inclined to respond positively: wasn't the Russian Revolution itself the outcome of diverse groups and demands (working class, peasants, middle class) that came together, with the working class becoming the umbrella standing for all? Traditional Marxists will accept that, but will explain that the leading role of the working class is because its position in the structure of society means it is destined to play this role. Then the question would be why such a revolution didn't happen where the working class was more advanced (e.g. Britain during industrialisation) and indeed why Marx didn't predict the Russian Revolution. This deserves some reflection.

I want to stress this point because it is a common line of attack against left populism: that populism moves away from a 'class analysis'. There is a truth in this argument, in the sense that populism makes the left consider other identifications beyond class rather than tying identity to a particular position determined by the relationship to the means of production. At the same time, however, populism allows us to rethink contemporary struggles, especially in contexts where the working class is defined more broadly, taking new forms and new roles that go beyond the white, male, industrial worker.

Having said that, it is important to acknowledge the context in which contemporary populist theory emerges and how it became a challenger to a class-centric analysis. For a long time 'populism' and 'class' have described very different political projects, especially for the left. Those like Ernesto Laclau and Chantal Mouffe, who later became the most well-known theorists of left populism, began their theory with a critique of traditional Marxism in the mid-1980s.

Their seminal book *Hegemony and Socialist Strategy* (1985) came after what is referred to as the 'cultural turn' – the theoretical and political opening that realised the importance of culture and identities for politics and, as I mentioned earlier, looked at politics beyond the formal institutions where it was exercised, as well as examining political identities beyond restricting them to class.

The first step in that direction had come much earlier with the work of the Italian Marxist Antonio Gramsci (1891–1937), who, despite remaining faithful to the economic analysis of his predecessors, realised that dominance in contemporary societies was achieved not only by coercion but with the 'ideological and moral leadership' exercised by the bourgeoisie, which he called 'hegemony'. This means that although the proletariat is still exploited, other mechanisms are in play that drive them to give consent to those in power.

The leadership of the dominant class presupposed the people's consent, which was achieved through cultural practices and with the creation of common ideological frames that promoted the interests of the bourgeoisie in more subtle ways. Part of that process also was the creation of a 'national interest' that would cut across class antagonisms in society and assist the dominant class. What Gramsci does here that is quite different from other Marxists is move the emphasis from economy (and the state) to civil society, thus paving the way for the importance of culture and identities in contemporary politics.

This expanded our understanding of what is political, and progressively – in academia but also in everyday politics – culture started to be part of the debates. This shift we call the 'cultural turn' and it was very much the product of the events of the 1960s, which put into question the ability of the existing communist parties to engage successfully with the uprisings of the time. The movements of 1968 were not (or not only) 'working class'. Many of those involved were members of the middle class, and they had demands that were not associated with labour conditions but life as a whole – from demanding a more democratic society, especially in the Eastern European bloc, to the end of the Vietnam War, for example.

The key moment that revealed the inability of the communist parties to comprehend these demands was the Soviet invasion of Prague in 1968, which assisted in creating splits in these parties across Europe. The central demand of the 'Prague Spring' had been a transition to democracy, and the subsequent military invasion led to protests around the world. Many communist parties across Europe (including the French and the Italian) denounced the invasion. The process of splitting from pro-Soviet parties which had started much earlier now reached countries like Greece. Although the reasons for the splits had their roots in disagreements beyond these events, they led to the formation of new communist parties like the Communist Party of Greece Interior (KKE interior) that followed less the example of the USSR and more a 'Eurocommunist' (and Gramscian) trajectory.

Another decisive moment in the 1960s was the tension between the social movements of May 1968 (especially in France) and the orthodox/traditional left, which dismissed them as 'middle-class' forms of 'identity politics'.[9] The key issue – still shaping many clashes on the left today – was the issue of political identities. Traditional Marxism saw these as the product of one's position in the relations of production. For this Marxist approach the economy was and remains the main determinant of all identities – class is what defines us and what differentiates our interests.

By moving away from Marxist economism, Laclau and Mouffe affirmed that political identities and political interests (and political struggles, by extension) were not predetermined or simply set by economics, but the product of contingent 'articulations'.

'Contingency' is a concept that invites a lot of criticism because it stands in opposition to 'necessity'.[10] Marxists, for example, will be on the side of necessity: the types of struggles (and revolutions) of the past and future have a 'necessary' character, and will take a particular form as Marx advocates: the capitalist system will unavoidably lead to the proletarianisation of the middle classes and then a proletarian mass will come head-to-head with the ruling class. Contingency

puts this narrative into question. It suggests that in particular historical conditions the emerging struggles will not follow a predetermined
plan, but a plan that would be shaped by the particularities of that
context. Does that mean that 'anything goes' and our political struggles
will be whimsical, accidental, submitted to the caprices of a destiny
void of meaning? No, not at all. It means that we should be open to
recognising the signs and opportunities of the historical moment we
are in, rather than believing in a predetermined destiny.

Within the particular contexts where struggles emerge, new ideological elements come together, new identities are forged and new
alliances are formed. The process rearranges the different elements
(ideas, practices, identities) and creates a new structured totality – we
call this 'articulation'.[11] Since it implies that nothing is given (or determined) *a priori*, this concept already puts theorists like Laclau and
Mouffe at odds with traditional Marxists. For the latter, this universe
of articulatory practices and contingency is at odds with the privileged role they assign to class and, by extension, economic position in
shaping identities and struggles.[12]

Since Laclau and Mouffe first advanced their critique some things
have changed: the importance of gender, race, religion and sexuality
have been incorporated into the demands of the left, and it seemed
that the debate about the centrality of class was receding. The movements following the financial crisis of 2007–8, however, brought the
discussion back to economic inequality, now focusing on the dis-
crepancy between the 99 per cent and the 1 per cent. 'Class' moved
back to the centre of contemporary debates, albeit not in the traditional sense. What I mean by that is that the working class has itself
changed. People with higher-education degrees (traditionally thought
of as middle class) are now on zero-hour contracts, placing them
among the most vulnerable of the working class, for example. How
class is defined is itself a product of a particular historical era. At the
same time, as economically focused demands started to re-emerge in
the context of the financial crisis, identity issues became the target of
right-wing populism. The gains of the past decades around gender,
religion, sexuality and race now started to be questioned. In August
2020, for example, President Trump called Black Lives Matter protesters 'thugs'. Paradoxically, renewed attacks on 'identity politics'
came also from a part of the left which remains faithful to traditional

Marxist analysis.[13] This part of the left, rather than reaffirming the importance of non-class identities and focusing on how class and race for example intersect, dismissed or tried to subsume the importance of identity under a class analysis.

Who's Afraid of Populism?

Beyond traditional Marxists, however, a whole army of scholars and commentators have been keen to show the dangers of populism – a populism understood in very different terms to what I have described here, and without engaging with Laclau and Mouffe's theoretical work. There are good reasons of course why so many, with so little knowledge on the subject, are willing to attack populism. On the one hand, it is the rise of right-wing populism, with leaders such as Donald Trump, Marine Le Pen and Boris Johnson. On the other, we are in the midst of a populism hype: the subject is hot and everyone feels compelled to write about it, even if they are new to the field. Other scholars are keen to defend liberal democracy by dismissing right and left populism by reaffirming the importance of existing institutions for a solution to contemporary ills. Müller is a case in point. Further, the same scholars seem to believe that populism theorists (that is, the ones who see populism as a way of doing politics rather than as an inherently dangerous phenomenon) fail to appreciate the merits of the existing institutional framework.

While critics of populism tend to bundle the left and right varieties together, I want to focus the discussion here on left populism. Left populism's defenders recognise that neoliberalism and technocracy lie behind the crisis of representation that we experienced with the financial crisis. The theorists, much like the parties associated with left populism such as Podemos and Syriza, are not necessarily opposed to the institutions of liberal democracy, although they would argue for their reform. As I argue in Chapter 5, neither Syriza nor Podemos seem to suggest a radical break with these institutions. Chantal Mouffe herself argues that 'the radical democratic conception of citizenship I am proposing is closely linked with the radical reformist politics of engagement with the institutions that I advocated earlier', that is, engagement with representative institutions in order to enhance economic rights and democratic representation. Mouffe's vision is underpinned by 'ethico-political principles of the liberal democratic *politeia*'.[14] In this respect left populism does not threaten the existing institutions other than with reform through more participatory practices.

At the same time some theorists (such as Laclau) believe, as I do, that populism can incorporate revolutionary politics and can be threatening to liberal institutions. For us 'populism' is one of the few ways of doing politics as a whole, a political logic if you like. What I mean by that is that most political projects (involving parties, movements, revolts, etc.) have a populist element in attempting to construct 'a people' which will stand against an enemy. This process can be successful or unsuccessful. The politics that do not do that are perpetuating institutional, technocratic or bureaucratic logics. For many theorists the focus is on the projects that attempt to reform the existing democratic institutions rather than destroy them (Chantal Mouffe often talks about that), making populism a radical reformist project which can remedy neoliberal societies. I don't see, however, why populism couldn't be a much more revolutionary project in a context that this would be desirable. Although I want to maintain that 'populist' politics could and should entail a more radical break with liberal democratic institutions, this is not something that will be decided *a priori* and there is definitely no blueprint of how far such 'radicalisation' could go.

Blair, Audience Democracy and Post-democratic Conditions

Earlier I referred to post-democratic conditions and the association of politics with technocracy that led to the crisis of representation after the financial crisis. During the 2019 electoral campaign in Britain, the ex-Prime Minister Tony Blair (responsible for contributing to the shift of social democratic parties closer to neoliberalism) decided to use the opportunity to enlighten us on 'populism', accusing both the Labour Party and the Conservatives of engaging in 'populism running riot'.[15] According to Blair the current populism of the two parties means 'peddling two sets of fantasies', and in this statement we can see that he implicitly equates populism with fantasy. 'Real' politics, for Blair, is to be found in the hallowed centre ground. What is striking in his interviews and statements is the total lack of reflection on his own contribution to this political conjuncture. The politics of Boris

Johnson and Jeremy Corbyn came at a time when the middle ground – made up of professional politicians who act like good technocrats taking care of matters that they assume the citizens cannot understand – had imploded.

This distance between those at the top of the political institutions and 'the people' is what some commentators call 'post-democracy'.[16] The politics of Blair's 'third way' (no left or right but only 'good' or 'bad' economics) in fact relied on this distance between institutions and people. This is not to say that Blair did not create a façade of being receptive to the demands of the people – it is well known that marketing and branding techniques were a big part of his premiership, including methods designed to find out how policies could be better 'sold' to voters (such as focus groups). This, however, maintains the people at a distance, as merely an audience.

The post-democratic condition has been cited as a reason for the recent rise of populist politics. The financial crisis of 2008 made the condition visible, including how it had eclipsed any form of citizens' participation in democratic politics.[17] The dominance of technocratic expertise in Western politics reduces democratic participation to a 'symbolic' (to use the anti-populist language) engagement with electoral politics every four to five years. Symbolic not only because it excludes continuous participation, but also because the choices on the menu for a long time offered no alternative to the neoliberal orthodoxy. As a result Western politics was reduced to a game between elected governments and elites that worked for the maximisation of business interests through structural reforms enabling market competitiveness. This 'distancing' between the people and power centres is achieved by two processes, which appear contradictory at first glance.

The first is bringing the people in, but only as spectators and audiences rather than as participants in the democratic process. For many scholars this development is associated with changes in political communication related to Western liberal democracies that go back at least to the 1980s, usually examined under the terms 'Americanisation' and 'professionalisation' of political communication. Borrowing from the fields of marketing and public relations, the development of techniques that treat citizens as consumers – in other words, selling them ideas and policies as if they were products – is seen as a distortion of the information and communication environment necessary for participatory democracy.[18]

This 'faux' involvement of the people as spectators has also been termed 'audience democracy', with the media assisting in the prioritisation of the image and especially the charismatic personality of the leader – their performance, their 'authenticity' – over and above the party, the programme and the vision of a better society.[19] This trend accelerated in the 1990s in Western democracies, and the selection of party leaders like Tony Blair in the UK and Bill Clinton in the US has been attributed to their ability to successfully manage their media image and to use marketing techniques in order to sell their message more effectively.

These changes, coupled with the increased distancing that is part of the post-democratic condition, are at the heart of the crisis of representation after the financial crisis of 2008.

The crisis in the countries of the European South had profound socio-economic effects and was experienced as a generalised crisis of social identities. It was not only the economy, not only the anger directed at those who had been representing us and led us to this situation; it was more as if each one and all of us unexpectedly felt the ground disappear beneath our feet. It was as if we all realised how fleeting any stability and safety, anything that we had taken as a given, really was. It may be that permanency and stability are always precarious, but the crisis brought this to the surface.

After the crisis many European countries (including Britain) experienced the detrimental effects of austerity, but nowhere else did it have such profound effects, cutting across classes, as it did in the European South and especially in Greece and Spain. That is why in these countries we saw the most forceful movements and activity at grassroots level, as well as a change in the dynamics of electoral politics. It is how 'the people' became determined to be heard.

What is it in this story that seems to disturb theorists so profoundly, commentators and politicians alike? What is it about the appearance of the people on the political scene that they find so threatening? They seem to concentrate their criticism on three areas: they question the claim of populists (parties or leaders) to be the representatives of the people; they question the idea of 'a people' itself; and they question the morality of it all. What they are saying, though it is concealed under the façade of theorising, is that when the people take centre stage, neo-liberal politics as we know it is under threat. If that is the case then, from a left-populist perspective, it is a blessing. While in reality the gains of left populism are only moderate at the time of writing, we can learn from these processes. That is the aim of this book.

What Is Populism?

Populism is not an easy concept to define. We have to examine how it operates in order to see why it attracts so much controversy from critics of so many different stripes. On the one hand, it seems to have an ambiguous relationship with ideology. On the other hand, it seems to have an ambiguous standing in concrete politics, challenging the liberal democratic institutions *and* rejecting a class analysis. What, then, is populism?

There are at least two ways of understanding populism. There are those who take a 'substantive' approach, associating populism with a particular content (an ideology or a set of policies, for example), and those who see populism more as a 'form', a way of doing politics – or better, one of the political logics that shape politics.[20] In the latter model populist politics is a logic, but this does not mean content or ideology are irrelevant. Although I agree that populism is a logic – the form that politics takes rather than its substance – the qualifiers 'right' or 'left' refer to the content this way of doing politics is taking in particular contexts. Content and ideology come in to differentiate between right and left populism.

Populism is defined by the condition that divides society, the polarisation between 'the people versus the elites'. The ideological content – the policies and the vision of society that different populisms advocate – is what differentiates between right and left. So right and left populisms have different content but populism is the form their politics take. Because populism is form, a political logic, accepting this definition in isolation, leads to the paradoxical argument that left and right populists are 'the same', since they are *both* proponents of 'pro-people and anti-elite politics'. This is not the case when the form is filled with the particular (left or right) content.

One of the commentators looking at populism as an ideology is Cas Mudde, who is one of the most prominent scholars on the subject in the public discourse. Mudde affirms the difficulties around the definition of populism 'without any qualifiers to become integrated in academic and popular debate'. But he also suggests 'that the academic community is closer to a consensus than it has ever been. Most scholars use populism as a set of ideas focused on an opposition between the people (good) and the elite (bad), although they still disagree on whether it is a fully fledged ideology or more a political discourse or style.'[21] His own conclusion is that populism is a 'thin-centred ideology'.[22] What he means is (1) that populism is an ideology and (2) that it is an ideology that borrows its content from other ideologies.

The person who coined the phrase 'thin-centred' ideology, Michael Freeden, will disagree, but before I go any further let us ponder the question of political ideologies. One definition is that a political ideology is a system of thought – sometimes more rigid, other times looser – through which individuals or groups of individuals understand the political world and act upon it. They are made up of concepts (but also beliefs, interpretations and even myths) that come together in particular (sometimes ambiguous or even contradictory) configurations.[23]

Ideologies are not very stable and as time goes by they are transformed or go through certain mutations. Think of liberalism for example: there was a core ideology defined by the work of John Stuart Mill, which consisted of the ideas of individual sovereignty, liberty (as the title of Mill's seminal work *On Liberty* suggests) and progress. Other concepts connect to these core ones, either closely or in a more peripheral manner.[24] This configuration could of course change over time or when associated with different political programmes.

So what are the concepts central to populism? Is it the concept of 'the people'? That alone doesn't say much about what populism stands for as an ideology or what one should do with these 'people'. Mudde tries to overcome this by calling it a 'thin-centred ideology', since because populism is more a way of doing politics (form) it lacks content. In this respect Mudde is right. Freeden will disagree because it's something that populism does systematically; it always relies on getting content from other ideological positions.[25]

Things become more clear, however, when we deal not with 'populism' as an ideology in itself but with right populism and left populism. The first will contain many of the core elements of ideologies such as conservatism (albeit in a new configuration) and the second elements from socialism/communism (again in a particular historical configuration). This plasticity of populism may suggest it is not an ideology (thin-centred or not) but rather a form, a logic and a way of doing politics that can be filled with different ideological content.

According to Laclau populism is a discursive strategy,[26] or as I prefer to call it a political logic: form rather than content. This means that populism is a way of doing politics, on both the left or the right. We can identify two main strategies or logics in politics. On the one hand, one allows us to do the type of politics that continue the already established institutional order (whatever that may be, from feudalism to liberal democracy). On the other hand, one does a different type of politics, one that is in an oppositional relationship with the established order, through the creation of 'a people' willing to stand against that order. This is neither a matter of style nor of ideological commitments. These come later.

It is worth remembering here that this is not the definition all theorists agree with. If one accepts populism as a logic which can take a revolutionary or reformist direction, the relationship with the existing institutions is a matter of degree. The emphasis is on the change it demands in the name of the people.

Let me return to the question of populism in contemporary politics more specifically. Laclau identifies two main political logics: populist and institutional. When we look at the particular historical expressions of populism we can identify failed or successful populist projects, but the basic grammar remains the same. Every revolution that involves a people against the existing institutions is based on this grammar, and every challenge to an established order by democratic means is also based on this grammar. How successful these challenges are is a different matter. In both cases you need 'a people' that will stand against the 'establishment'. This 'people' can be defined as the 'working class', 'the 99 per cent' or some other name, but it is 'a people' that will challenge the status quo. To put it another way, populism is inseparable from the idea of antagonism.

The political field in populism is separated into two antagonistic camps ('us' and 'them', or 'the people' versus 'the establishment') where the former advance demands that interrupt 'politics as usual'. This is equally true for left and right populism. Trump was as much an interruption in these terms for the US as Podemos was for Spain.

The feeling of an interruption is what unsettles commentators on populism, especially the ones who are afraid of the effect of populism on liberal institutions. In more theoretical terms, the objections to populism seem to gravitate around three areas: political representation, the status of 'the people' and the morality of populism or, better, the morality of populist leaders who are seen as ruthless manipulators of the masses.

In this vein Müller and others argue that those claiming to be the 'true representatives of the people' not only represent a people that doesn't exist but also try to give a moralistic dimension to their politics. They insist that populism rests on 'the moralistic imagination of politics'[27] and populist leaders always seem to project their moral purity and authenticity when they claim to 'talk the truth'. Müller has put his finger on something, but he is too keen to fault 'populists' (including left populists).

It is true that often left populists operate in terms of how the world should be and they take a stance against those on power – this is what change is all about: not only looking at how politics are but also how politics should be and how they should be different than the politics of the 'elites'. In theoretical terms, what Müller may point to unintentionally with the term 'morality' is not a set of historically and socially specific rules but rather a framework created by a mixture of how things ought to be and some rules we have absorbed through our practical engagement with the world as it is. These dimensions can be an important aspect of populist politics. Since populist politics is the opposite of following the institutional establishment it must entail a vision of how the world should be in the future, and this will differentiate it from 'politics as usual'.[28]

Both left and right populists are a challenge to what is thought of as the status quo in a particular context, and what is thought of as 'the establishment', and in that sense their ability to convince rests on having a vision of how things ought to be – this is the normative dimension of populism. Let us, however, differentiate between this dimension and a utopian dimension. Although populism is about how things should be, it is nevertheless connected with the 'real' dimension of politics, politics as they are. After all, populism emerges from a set of very real demands, demands grounded on the here and now and at the same time aspiring for something better.

We have to accept that what makes populism a successful political project is the combination of elements from both dimensions, that is, the normative and the 'real' dimensions of politics. It is an intervention in contemporary politics that combines a description of what has gone wrong and how it can be put right with a vision for the future. The connection between the two is what Laclau calls an 'ethical investment',[29] an investment that brings to the forefront the emotive or affective side of politics.

Left Populism

The affective (or emotive) dimension of populism is quite evident in both right and left populism. Populists leaders address their publics in a more emotive way, and similarly 'the people' themselves seem to become more emotive, more determined to win for their side and ready to make sacrifices. This is also why they are perceived as dangerous for those attached to the routine continuity of non-populist politics.

The connection between real politics and normative politics is important for challenging 'politics as usual'. This connection is part and parcel of the left: each strike, each demonstration is not only about the particular issue at hand. It is also a step forward, a contribution to a much bigger struggle aiming to change the system as a whole.

There is a paradox here: the left accepting the broad framework of democratic politics as we know it, while at the same time aspiring to challenge and change the very same politics, can tilt the scale towards very moderate reforms and then we have a further debate over how 'left' the left is.

The problems, however, start when the differences between right and left populism are obscured. Earlier on I mentioned that some theorists define populism as an ideology – even if it is only a 'thin-centred' one, as Mudde insists. Populism is a logic at the theoretical level, but in concrete politics it is filled with a particular content, a content that can be right or left wing. Ideologies, as a set of political ideas and values, are differentiated from one another according to the core and peripheral principles on which they rest. It is these ideas and values that provide the content, rather than populism as a political logic.

Although the operations of a populist logic can work for either the right or the left, when we turn to the content of particular political projects we can clearly distinguish between a left-populist project and a right-populist one.

A right-populist project will usually contain one or more of the following: conservative social values, market liberalism, individualism and nationalism. A left-populist project may emphasise communitarianism and equality. Some left-populist projects may be based on bureaucratic centralism or on democratic socialism, others not. There are, however, particular characteristics that will define a left-populist project. These include enhancement of political participation and inclusivity. It is the failure to recognise these differences that inhibits the emergence and development of a left-populist project fit for the twenty-first century.

Earlier, when discussing the logic of equivalence, this was aligned with the process of bringing demands together. The difference between left and right lies in the content of the demands brought together. In both cases we see the characteristic division of the political space into two antagonistic camps. But only by examining the concrete demands that come together can we differentiate between left-populist and right-populist projects. It's worth remembering that in the logic of equivalence we have the unification of diverse struggles, and this unification enables a decisive challenge to the establishment to emerge. As I mentioned earlier, the chain of equivalence is a chain and not a mass because something of the differences of these demands remains, even when they are united in a chain.

To be fair, this is often how the traditional left approached politics too. They did this by uniting different demands under the banner of 'the working class', and sometimes it succeeded. Craig Calhoun, in his critique of E. P. Thompson's *The Making of the English Working Class*, showed that there were many heterogeneous groups which were all united under the banner 'working class' radicalism during the nineteenth century.[30]

In the new millennium, however, the problem is the 'reformism' of left politics. A number of left parties, as Mouffe notes,[31] have tried to discard their left identity, redefining themselves as 'centre-left' and in many cases pursuing policies enabling neoliberalism (starting with Tony Blair's Labour Party in the late 1990s). This neoliberalism, implemented in an increasingly technocratic manner that alienated their historical base, is one of the reasons behind the crisis of representation after the 2008 financial crisis and why a contemporary political intervention has to reconnect and redefine, but definitely avoid discarding, a left identity.

The difference between a left-populist project and a centre-left non-populist one is that instead of the logic of equivalence I mentioned earlier, we have a different operation: a logic of difference whereby the political space becomes more complex through a proliferation of demands that do not separate the political field into two antagonistic camps. The system will manage to absorb these demands and struggles, or eliminate them separately. This would also explain another attack by Müller: charging populists with being anti-pluralists while also questioning populism's commitment to enhancing grassroots participation.[32] The anti-pluralist accusation goes back to these two logics: equivalence and difference. For those afraid that populism will make the liberal democratic institutions redundant, populism seems to divide the political space in an undesirable way. In a non-populist era the system can manage the diverse demands one by one (by satisfying or discarding them) because they remain unconnected.

The distinction between left and right points to a dichotomy that is part of a particular kind of universe: a universe composed of divergent entities which oppose each other. The contrast between the two involves not only different ideologies but very different solutions to everyday problems that lead to oppositional programmes.[33] There are parties that seem to transcend this left–right dichotomy – for example, Bobbio mentions the Green parties.[34] That is, parties dealing with issues and solutions that wouldn't be acceptable for only the left or the right. I have to say, however, that in my view the left–right distinction is very much alive. Take the Green parties for example: as climate change becomes the most pressuring political problem and there is increased resistance from power centres, it becomes very much a 'left', anti-capitalist issue.

Right-wing populists go out of their way to deny the mere existence of climate change and the traditional right seems more comfortable with responses based on individual responsibility (as individuals or companies) rather than suggesting radical structural adjustments. In this context I believe Green parties will move to the left and left parties will have to incorporate the environment into their lists of priorities. This is what happened with the Labour Party and is significant in understanding how contemporary political parties change their priorities and go beyond the traditional distinctions.

The left–right distinction, however, is not only associated with parties and electoral politics but also with movements, movements that Bobbio argues cannot be categorised by their position in this distinction.[35] This is true not only because the identity of movements goes beyond party identification but also because the interests and demands expressed in these movements can be left or right, diverse and contradictory. As I mentioned earlier though, the movements are the ground where grievances start to come together for the creation of 'a people', and this is why they need to be examined as part of right or left populism for the purpose of this discussion.

The Indignados movement (or 'Movement of the Squares') in Greece and Spain is a good example of how contemporary demands are expressed beyond the traditional left framework. These demands, even when associated with economic grievances, go further than that: they are demands for a different democratic model. Furthermore, they are demands that cut across class lines.

Left Populism: Transversality, Inclusivity, Internationalism

Going beyond the left–right distinction is what most social democratic parties did with catastrophic effects, and in a different way it is also one of the accusations against contemporary left-populist parties. This is associated with one of the strategies of left populism: transversality. Transversality refers to a type of cutting across left and right – but this time in order to redefine the political field rather than occupy the middle ground and end up with a moderate reformism. Transversality in populism is rearranging the board, it is a strategy that enables one to appeal beyond those who already embrace left politics. The aim is to construct 'the people', not to triangulate to the political centre. Transversality and inclusivity are characteristic of certain contemporary left-populist projects.

Let's use an example from contemporary politics. In order to create a new, powerful antagonism with the established order of neoliberalism, the Spanish left-populist party Podemos found a strategic advantage in the concept of transversality. Note that I call it left despite its transversal strategy. For them, transversality enabled them to mark an end to the old Spanish politics of left or right, and instead create an antagonistic frontier between the establishment and the people.

The concept of transversality can signify the need to change the rules of the political game and leave behind the old political categories. Put another way, transversality is about changing the terms of what we are struggling about and for – and making sure that those terms favour the way *we* see the world.

This is one of the aims of left populism. It is different from right populism because it has another very important characteristic: it is inclusive. The antagonist is not determined according to religion, race, nationality or gender but by something entirely different. This is what the Occupy movement tried to capture in the slogan 'We are the 99 per cent'. And it is difficult to think of a more 'left' project than pitching the 99 per cent against the top 1 per cent! Left populism recognises that we belong on the same side, irrespective of our race, ethnicity, sexuality or religion. It does not (or it should not) exclude from 'the people' anyone but the powerful and the super-wealthy.

If left populism is inclusive it goes without saying that it cannot put the 'nation', 'race' or religion at its core. Having said that, this discussion is a bit more complicated as there have been past and present projects claiming to be left populist that tried to incorporate aspects of nationalism, one of the latest examples which enjoyed momentary success being that of Jean-Luc Mélenchon in France.

There are two aspects that we should be aware of here. First, the case of Mélenchon has to be contextualised with references to the role of the nation in the French Republic (which is beyond the scope of this book). When 'the nation' becomes an element of a left-populist programme it may use the demand for 'national sovereignty' against supranational institutions that have been occupied by neoliberal forces, but it should also entail the potential for a necessary, broader political project of resistance, one that brings together the demands of different people(s) beyond national frontiers. Mélenchon failed to entertain such an inspiration; instead his project remained very much tainted by a (perhaps not explicit) latent nationalism.

Second, 'the nation' could also be central in left-populist projects in South America (in Venezuela for example), which enables them to stand against a clearly defined imperial power, in this case the US.

Within the European context (and especially in relation to imperial powers like France or Great Britain), nationalism is more problematic as it tends to exclude exactly those that left populism should embrace. The discussion between one of the key figures of Podemos, Íñigo Errejón, and the political theorist Chantal Mouffe is quite illuminating on the possibility of a national left populism.[36] Errejón characterises the Latin American experience as a situation where large popular sectors that had been previously excluded from economic and political power by oligarchies demanded their inclusion and integration into the 'nation', and this demand in context is a radical one. In the European context, however, despite all sort of exclusions, some level of democratisation is more prominent. I discuss nationalism and the nation state further in Chapter 6 when I turn to the issue of Brexit.

A left-populist strategy worth the name cannot follow the path of the right-wing populists. Inclusivity and internationalism should be central to any left-populist project.[37] We are past the point where any of our contemporary evils, from financialisation to climate change, can be remedied by isolated nations.

Political Lessons from Left Populism

I hope that in this chapter I have shown how populism operates, and how it produces 'a people' that is not predetermined and shaped around class lines but which still retains a radicality, and allows us to understand how contemporary struggles can also be formed around other categories such as race or ethnicity. This becomes more pressing when we note that the financial crisis happened alongside refugee flows from the Middle East, which for the populist right enabled convenient scapegoating.

Although populism operates in a particular way, by dividing the political space into two antagonistic camps and by bringing 'a people' to the forefront, the content of right and left populism is different, both in terms of actual political programmes and the political visions each aspires to realise. As discussed in the previous section, left populism has to be transversal, inclusive and internationalist. Despite national elements being part of left-populist projects in South America, in the European context left populism should steer clear of nationalism.

If we compare left populism with the traditional left there are many differences (not least that class becomes one among many possible ways of promoting a left project), but it would be in the interests of anyone who wants to overcome neoliberalism to take into account the historical conditions that gave relevance to contemporary left populism, not least the collapse of the Eastern European bloc.

If we compare left-populist parties with the social democratic parties which declined after the 2008 financial crisis when left-populist parties started to gain ground (unfortunately not for long), we can again see an important difference. The social democratic parties had become 'catch-all' parties rather than populist parties, which did not allow them to deal successfully with the crisis. 'Catch-all' parties and populist parties are not the same. The former tried to become friends to all, enemies to none, while at the same time distancing themselves from the people rather than bringing to the forefront 'a people'. They created a distance from both their voters and their own grassroots and promoted the idea that politics should be left to 'expert' technocrats. When the crisis hit, the people returned with a vengeance and questioned all expertise, given that the financial 'experts' had failed so flagrantly. The social democrats were in no position to respond because they had embraced the neoliberal paradigm of the past 40 years rather than challenging it.

I have argued that part of populism is the operation of bringing together diverse demands, a chain of equivalence. However, this chain cannot expand indefinitely. If the expansion of the chain starts to incorporate elements of the 'establishment' then it not only starts to lose vigour, but it ends up resembling the 'catch-all' parties. Some of the parties I examine later on seem to have committed exactly this, but again we have to make a number of theoretical and strategic differentiations on that level too.

The aim of European left populism should be the transformation of the democratic institutions towards a radical, participatory alternative. The direction of these left-populist programmes should come from 'the people'. And the first appearance of the people after the crisis was in the movements that demanded a new political and economic alternative.

2

Grassroots Resistance, Austerity and the 'Populist Moment'

It is not only populism that many authors find difficult to identify in specific terms. The same is also true for the concept of a 'movement': any demonstration, any march, any grassroots activity becomes a 'movement', in many cases because the term gives greater significance to such activity. One thing that differentiates a movement from a one-off protest is its duration. There was not a sustained movement against austerity in the UK in the same way there was in Greece and Spain, which is not to suggest that some UK organisations didn't work continuously against austerity.

As for a 'populist' movement, the reality is that UK austerity, despite its devastating effects, never cut across social classes in the immediate and devastating way that it did in Southern Europe, where the financial crisis created a number of responses, from riots to single demonstrations to movements. What is significant, however, is that in some of these cases, mainly the Indignados movement of 2011 in Spain and Greece, we have the first coming together of diverse demands that later became the basis for the electoral projects of Podemos and Syriza respectively. Similar attempts like the Occupy movement (despite its international character) it is less clear if it had an impact on electoral politics and the Bernie Sanders presidential campaign (won by Hillary Clinton who became the Democratic Party nominee) in 2016. Why we look at these movements in relation to left populism is not only because they are the ground for the first 'coming together' of a people, but also because when left-populist parties lose this connection with the grassroots they seem to be unable to bring about a more radical alternative to existing institutions, even if they win elections. I examine this in more depth in the following chapters.

UK anti-austerity activism, despite inspiring and educating a new generation of activists, did not bring the diverse demands together in a left-populist project. In June 2015 a wide range of UK grassroots organisations and campaigns, organised around the People's Assembly, called for a march against austerity, which mobilised around 250,000 people. The crowd was addressed by Jeremy Corbyn (at that point a Labour Party leadership candidate), Green leader Caroline Lucas, union leaders and many others, including myself as a Syriza activist. It was one of the high times of British radical politics, before Brexit dominated every political discussion, and enabled many writers to celebrate the anti-austerity 'movement' in Britain.[1]

According to the figures of a 2017 study on government spending and mortality, an estimated 120,000 more people have died in the UK due to government austerity cuts than predicted by previous mortality trends.[2] Demonstrations had also been called in previous years by the TUC, for example in 2011. Although there were a number of smaller mobilisations supporting Greece, many of which were called by the Greece Solidarity Campaign, and some activity by groups such as UK Uncut, People's Assembly and others, we should be sceptical of claims that marches in themselves are sufficient to constitute a movement. We could argue that the UK anti-austerity organisations were connected with the international movement against austerity, although the connections with them were more symbolic than anything else. At that march I addressed the protesters as a spokesperson of Syriza, but after Syriza signed the memorandum later that summer many of the organisations behind the demo lost interest in their politics.

How we view this activity will depend of course on how we define a social movement, especially within the context of the new social movements that emerged after the 1960s. For some theorists, as I discuss later, movements express universalist concerns, often protesting in the name of morality rather than the direct interests of a particular social group. In this respect anti-austerity movements across the world would fit the definition as austerity did cut across classes. On this view social movements are oriented towards civil society rather than the state, which would be problematic for the anti-austerity movements although they can be seen as aiming at changing the common frames that justify austerity ('if you spend you have to pay'); and their organisation is 'informal' and 'loose' – during 2015 most people in the UK engaged with anti-austerity via other organisations (unions, non-governmental organisations (NGOs), etc.), but this is also part of how movements come into being.[3] What is more problematic for me in the UK case, however, is that a movement – any type of movement – must have some duration, and although some of the organisations involved in the anti-austerity movement still go on this is relevant for only a very small number of activists.

The bigger problem, however, is that in the last few years the definition of a movement has been used to describe any grassroots activity that enjoys some popularity: Momentum is a movement, and even Golden Dawn (the Nazi Greek party) has been referred to me as a movement. I would therefore reserve the term for political activity that involves formal organisations and more flexible forms of membership, whose composition exhibits some relative diversity and which has some duration (it might only last a few months but it could be longer). In terms of the British anti-austerity movement, it may be that we are not dealing with a social movement at all but rather with a labour movement.

Even if one is willing to go with the position that there was an anti-austerity movement in Britain circa 2015, a number of further questions arise. Did this movement have a wider objective, to change attitudes towards the economy for example, or was it only interested in electing an anti-austerity leader who could address inequality from a position of power? And why was this movement only moderately successful in electoral terms in the 2017 election and ultimately unable to secure a Corbyn victory? If movements have electoral objectives, was this movement (if we agree to call it that) an unsuccessful movement? According to Jeremy Corbyn the argument was won,[4] but one could argue that the change in right-wing politics may have had a role to play in that. This does not mean that the cuts all stopped, still less were reversed, but that the right-wing discourse changed, focusing on nation, race, etc.

Furthermore, the reason why there was no Labour electoral victory may at least partially be attributed to Brexit. Finally, like the Greek and Spanish cases, Jeremy Corbyn also seemed to lose progressively the connection with the wider grassroots of the party (attacks from the right played a role in that), despite the vitality of Momentum, the group springing out of his leadership campaign.

While Greece and Spain, in their particular context framed by their membership of the eurozone, had diverse and vibrant movements which enabled the transportation of the demands of the people to the electoral level, the British case is less clear cut but also a very interesting example of how populist strategy could potentially work in different contexts. The relationship between movements and parties can be a fruitful starting point for understanding the politics of Europe after the crisis – South (Greece and Spain) and North (Britain) – and by extension populism.[5] Let's examine closer the developments of Southern Europe. In the PIGS countries (Portugal, Italy, Greece and Spain), all members of the eurozone, the inability to pay government debt or bail out indebted banks saw these countries forced into a regime of severe austerity by the combined forces of their governments, the ECB and the IMF. The European elites advanced a narrative that blamed the affected countries for 'imprudent' fiscal policies responsible for their deficits – namely their levels of public spending. Austerity and cuts, however, did not only apply to the public sector but also to the private. As lower incomes and the property of the lower to middle class were heavily taxed, the working classes were reduced to pauperisation and the middle classes started to collapse. Greece and Spain became the most prominent cases of austerity in Europe and by 2013 Greece was thirteenth and Spain eleventh (among 90 countries) in the Global Misery Index Scores.[6]

Between 2010 and 2015 the crisis and the successive Troika bailouts that enforced austerity on Greece had devastating effects. Between 2009 and 2013 unemployment increased from 9.5 per cent to 27.9 per cent. During the same period average wages decreased by almost 40 per cent and pensions by 45 per cent. By 2013 over 44 per cent of the Greek population had an income below the poverty line. After austerity measures were introduced, health services totally deteriorated and millions were excluded from the healthcare system. During the first two years of austerity the suicide rates increased by 35 per cent and depression rates almost tripled.

Similarly, in Spain the unemployment rate increased from 11.3 per cent in 2008 to 21.6 per cent in 2011. Public debt showed a dramatic rise, increasing by almost 70 per cent between 2008 and 2011 to reach 736,468 million euros. Although gross domestic product (GDP) had staged something of a recovery by 2011, inflation, as measured by consumer prices, increased by five percentage points between 2008 and 2011.[7]

From the start of the crisis grassroots activity and collective action started to grow, but it is worth exploring the different forms of this activity further and their later contribution to left populism in electoral terms. The relationship between grassroots activity, social movements and populism is a significant part of the populist debate for two main reasons. First, the contribution to populist theory goes back to the challenge of the strict economism of traditional Marxists, as I mentioned in Chapter 1. Some of the movements that emerged from the crisis were challenging not only the economics of the crisis but political representation as such, and populism, left and right, is often a response to a broader crisis of representation. Second, following from the previous point, we can argue that a 'people's populism', a radical democratic populism – a left populism that starts from the grassroots level – demands that rather than focusing on a populist leader or a party's electoral strategy, we start from the bottom (from civil society), where demands are first formed and 'a people' becomes a possibility.

Let's start with a typology of social movements and especially the movements emerging after the financial crisis. Some argue that these constituted a new global phenomenon and a new type of mass mobilisation,[8] while others treat them as a reaffirmation of the importance of the older labour movements (in the sense that they addressed grievances such as inequality). Finally, there are those who advance a thesis that challenges the division between social movements and labour movements.[9] The division between labour movements and social movements is a significant one because for a long time it has underpinned different trajectories in left politics, mapped according to the theoretical lines discussed in Chapter 1. It would also explain the difference between the anti-austerity movement in Greece and Spain on the one hand, and the movement in Britain. Labour movements sit comfortably within traditional Marxism, while social movements are more of a focus for post-Marxists and those interested in populism.

For scholars of social movements the post-financial crisis movements are important because they can be presented as a 'new global movement phenomenon'.[10] In academia, in publishing and in advertising whatever claims to be 'new' (with at least some justification) has the potential for success. The problem with this attitude is that diverse 'movements' were grouped under the same banner (especially when the common thread is the use of social media that enabled the organisation of these movements) and less attention was paid to the different contexts, demands and ultimately outcomes.

The difficulties of addressing the anti-austerity movements associated with the financial crisis do not stop there though. The definition of what constitutes a movement, for example how it differs from protests or riots, is also a point of contestation. Broadly speaking a social movement will have some concern with culture and identity as opposed to focusing on strictly economic demands, and in terms of organisation it will be more flexible, more informal and, in many cases, more horizontal than at least some of the labour/trade union movements.[11] It will have a longer duration than a protest or a riot, the focus will not be on the participants' violence (although violence can be part of the protesters' repertoire)[12] and its composition may involve diverse organisations, individuals and classes (as opposed to protests organised by a single political party, trade unions, etc.). That definition does not exclude the involvement of unions and parties in a broader movement.

In relation to populism (to put it somewhat crudely), movements are the moment when diverse demands start to come together and 'a people' starts to emerge opposing an 'establishment' or the political elites more broadly: *la casta* in the case of the Spanish Indignados movement, a memorandum in the case of the Greek indignant/Aganaktismenoi movement. These elements were more pronounced in the Indignados movements in Greece and Spain. In the case of Greece, though, I want to start earlier: in December 2008 when the murder of a young anarchist by a police officer led to weeks of extensive rioting – a type of collective response that has many similarities with the London riots. Are these two instances disassociated from the context of the crisis or are they the first responses to an increasingly asphyxiating environment, politically, economically and socially? Greek activists themselves, interviewed a couple of years after the events, would argue for the latter. I have included some material from these interviews in the section on the riots of December 2008 and I provide some direct quotes that I think bring to life the feelings of activists during these events.

Violence, Emotions and 'Acting Out'

At Exarchia, the anarchist/left hub in downtown Athens, a commemorative plaque has been erected where 15-year-old Alexandros

Grigoropoulos was killed in 2008 by a police officer. Next to this plaque there is another for 15-year-old Berkin Elvan, killed during the anti-government protests in Turkey in 2014. Apart from having the same age, the two young men were victims of police brutality and authoritarianism. Their depiction side by side creates an affinity between anti-government protests in different parts of the world, and in this way they both participate in a unified narrative against authoritarianism and oppression. Despite the different contexts, these two murders sparked widespread demonstrations and riots. During the time of the European crisis another well-known event that led to widespread rioting was the death of Mark Duggan in London in 2011. These cases together pose the question of collective action and the crisis. Were these cases connected with the experience of the financial crisis in the respective countries? Do we learn anything from these early reactions, about the different types of grievances that lead to the articulation of a chain with the potential of leading to a left-populist project?

In order to answer these questions I focus first on the 2011 London riots and then on the 2008 Greek riots in order to compare them with other types of mobilisation during the course of the crisis. Although these cases are not often seen as movements per se but more as explosions of sentiment leading to violence, these forms of collective action do foreground more conscious demands like the ones we find in movements. Movements do not spark out of thin air. They are built on previous mobilisations that create what some call 'submerged networks'[13] that could form the basis of collective action at a later time. The London riots have been connected by some commentators with the deprivation experienced by some communities in Britain, especially after the financial crisis began. Violence was the main media frame of the events of August 2011, a reaction to the death of the mixed heritage 29-year-old Mark Duggan in Tottenham, London. The victim was shot on 4 August by a specialised armed unit after being stopped while in a taxi. The unit was investigating gun crime but the exact circumstances are unclear and disputed. The police certainly released false information which was challenged by the Black Independent Advisory Group monitoring policing in the area. Activists and Duggan's friends and family (200–300 people according to media reports) gathered outside Tottenham police station on 6 August. Soon a dispute started between the protesters and the police, and violence started first in Tottenham and over the next couple of days spread to Enfield, Brixton, Hackney, Clapham, Croydon and other London locations.

By 8 and 9 August the violence had spread to Birmingham, Manchester, Nottingham and Liverpool. It focused around looting shops, attacking police stations and burning vehicles. The media used the term 'copycat criminality' and the then Prime Minister David Cameron talked about 'criminality pure and simple'.[14] According to statistical information from the Ministry of Justice, by early September 2011 4,000 people had been arrested. According to the same source, although there was the assumption that violence was gang related, only 13 per cent of those arrested had a gang affiliation.[15] It has also been disputed whether the riots can be characterised as 'ethnic' since they were ethnically heterogeneous and one-third of those arrested were white.[16]

Within the British context, as some scholars argue, the 2011 riots were different from the Brixton riots in 1981. Although in 2011 the black population was overrepresented in the riots, their presence was significantly less than at the Brixton riots 30 years earlier.[17] What some research suggests, however, is that in areas 'where police had worse relations with the public, rioting against the police attracted less disapproval from the local community. Certainly there is strong evidence that anger at the police was not simply a rationalisation proffered by rioters.'[18] Furthermore, a number of scholars find a link between deprivation (including recessions) and rioting.[19] One rioter summarised the reasons behind the London riots as follows: 'We hate the police, hate the government, got no opportunities [...] I became involved in the riots in Salford because it was a chance to tell the police, tell the government, and tell everyone else for that matter that we get fucking hacked off around here and we won't stand for it.'[20]

We can than allege that the exclusion of certain communities, black but also white, played a significant role in making the death of Duggan the emblem of many excluded communities in the UK which finally let their rage out. This rage was later expressed in a populist project but not a left-wing one. As far as I know the British left was not part of nor had a prominent place in the 2011 riots. Diverse grievances did however come together creating 'a people' later, leading to the Brexit vote. Going back to the 2015 anti-austerity movement in Britain, the analysis of the 2011 riots would suggest that the financial crisis was experienced mainly by communities which had already been deprived and excluded for decades. Rather than the cross-sector economic but also political demands at national level in Greece and Spain, the expression of political dissatisfaction in Britain mainly targeted the EU.

The Greek riots of December 2008, on the other hand, brought together the country's original organisers of the indignant movement. It has been argued that these networks were the basis of the anti-austerity protests in the case of Greece,[21] but from December 2008 we saw the incorporation of new social groups (young people) and an even greater horizontal expansion in the Greek indignant movement in 2011.

The shock of the crisis, the realisation of the extent of the risks taken by the financial sector with little consideration for the public, the permissiveness of the governments and the use of public money to bail out those who were responsible for the crisis in the first place may have contributed to the riots – but not yet as a conscious reaction to what was going on. In Britain this more explicit opposition towards finance took the form of the Occupy movement. Similarly, in Greece, despite the link between the 2008 riots and the crisis, the reaction to the death of Grigoropoulos was not consciously connected with the crisis. It took a while before the situation sank in and was expressed more consciously almost three years later with the indignant movement.

The Greek riots started with another death and they echoed similar beginnings in diverse contexts, from Europe to the Arab Spring. On 6 December 2008 a police officer shot Alexandros Grigoropoulos, a 15-year-old anarchist in Exarchia, a neighbourhood at the centre of Athens designated as a hub for anarchist and leftist groups. In retrospect, given that the policeman, Epaminondas Korkoneas, originally received a life sentence but was then released in 2019 in recognition of a 'prior honourable life', the demand for 'justice' that directed the extensive violence against symbols of the capitalist state (banks, big corporations, police stations, etc.) was well placed.

It was not the first time that Greek police had murdered innocent minors who were perceived to be a 'threat' to the establishment, and the similarities between Grigoropoulos and the murder of 15-year-old Michalis Kaltezas in 1985 by another policeman, who again was soon set free by the Greek justice system, were striking. And it was not only these cases. According to the people involved in the events that followed from the first night:

> In the last ten years more than 200–300 immigrants have been killed by the police [...] there are also other cases similar to Grigoropoulos – the young Maragopoulos, the gypsies killed in Menidi [...] But Grigoropoulos was Greek, white, the child of a middle-class family, it happened inside Exarchia. (Giannis, 33)[22]

The significance of Exarchia is as important as the profile of the victim. As a place of resistance, an armed attack against a young anarchist inside the neighbourhood immediately mobilised people in the area (hanging out in the many bars and restaurants of the area or living there), whose identity is broadly constructed as 'anti-establishment'. The profile of Grigoropoulos led to further mobilisations at schools, which significantly expanded the scope of the protests. Soon the events spread all over Athens and to other cities, even to areas that have little history of resistance.

The forms of action varied from protests and attacks to sit-ins, expressing not only the expected rage against the establishment and particularly the institutions of state oppression and justice but a more generalised discontent. The images of riots and burned buildings (as well as riot police protecting the Christmas tree at Syntagma Square, in front of the Greek Parliament in Athens) travelled around the world. The media love a good picture and a story that 'bleeds', but for those familiar with mass mobilisations violence was only one aspect of the repertoire of collective action, exploited to the full by the Greek mass media. After the first few days the duration of the protests and the diversity of the grievances expressed suggests that the death of young Grigoropoulos brought to the surface anger towards the chronic structural deficiencies of the Greek state – the types of deficiencies that contributed to Greece's vulnerability when the crisis struck. One of the activists I interviewed back then, Ririka, a young woman of 35, said:

After the first days things changed. The debates were about poverty, corruption. During December the Ministry of Employment was occupied [...] People started to think their position towards more general things, all were now annoyed with the Greek reality of nepotism and clientelism, the word 'justice' was everywhere, even for those who were not politicised.

The question in both cases (Greece 2008 and London 2011) is how to understand the motivation behind them. Not only the immediate motivation – the police murders themselves – but the direct connection with injustices (police brutality and oppression directed at specific communities, racial or 'ideological') and the questions of unconscious motivation that go beyond that. Looting and violence, and the absence of overarching articulated demands, often obscure the potential causes behind these events.

In the case of the London riots, media narratives ignored the anger accumulated by communities that had for decades been victimised and excluded from the benefits of globalisation. The riots, however, revealed the huge divisions that existed within the metropolitan space; and the widespread failure to recognise their political significance only served to further underline the marginalisation of those involved. In the case of December 2008, when I interviewed participants a few years later,[23] the effects of the financial crisis had already struck Greece with the greatest severity.

Ironically, for the first couple of years the crisis was dismissed as 'irrelevant for a small country like Greece' by part of the public, according to my interviewees. It was only in 2010, when the then Prime Minister George Papandreou (leader of PASOK, the social democratic party which has since declined significantly) announced that Greece would be subjected to the lending mechanisms of the Troika, that the extent of the crisis for Greece started to sink in. In the interviews related to the December 2008 events, many of the interviewees argued that a significant reason for the 2008 mobilisations was the underlying (even 'unconscious') economic pressure and political disillusionment with the establishment. This was amplified by a range of domestic economic scandals and constitutional and legal changes (such as the constitutional revisions abolishing the article specifying that Greek higher education is free and public, which was a factor in the student mobilisations of 2006–7).[24]

Many interviewees said that most people had already started to feel a generalised pressure, a sense of 'suffocation', which at that point could not be directly attributed to the impeding economic and political crisis. It is not uncommon when we recall events to create a coherent structure, where everything comes together in a rational tapestry, and that may be the case here. At the same time, in politics as in life, individually or collectively, our motivations and our actions are not always the product of fully conscious and rational choices.

Despite the intensity, violence and in the Greek case duration of the mobilisation, in both cases things returned to normal afterwards. They may have contributed to rendering visible certain injustices and deficiencies, they may even have politicised some groups, contributing to the further enlargement of submerged networks, but they didn't articulated a clear challenge to power centres.

When it came to the financial crisis, the protest movements appeared as different instances sometime afterwards. This time lag could be because it took time for the effects to be felt, or because the people didn't realise immediately that the measures imposed by governments were directed against the people themselves and that they would have long-lasting effects on their lives.

Having said that, it is also true that in our personal lives as in our political lives we react to things without being conscious of what we react to. Psychoanalysts use the term 'acting out' in order to describe these discharges by means of action – this type of letting off steam that is not yet directed to those responsible for the situation but is a less processed reaction directed at experiences of 'injustice'. The concept refers to repressed material that bubbles up in the form of behaviour that can be forceful and not quite make sense. As such, this type of behaviour can easily be characterised as impulsive and not in line with how the particular person or persons used to behave. Jacques Lacan, a well-known psychoanalyst and theorist, explains how this impulsive behaviour is an attempt to 'correct' something in the social order (symbolic order in Lacan). Thus it demands some interpretation.[25] This sense of generalised injustice that perpetuates all aspects of Greek society, and this sense of suffocation that the interviewees described, was partly expressed through a 'cry' (in some cases literally as one participant recalls), which then turned into the violence of December: 'When I realised what had happened I went out on the balcony and started screaming' (Nikos, 35).

The media often connect these 'acting-out' actions with teenagers, but age is not a shield against the bottling up of emotions and the 'not consciously targeting' release – except, I assume, if one is a developmental psychologist.

In terms of populism, however, these events, and the 'submerged networks' that seem to expand in these processes of collective action, contain the potential to transform into what I called in Chapter 1 an 'equivalence chain'; in the vernacular the linking of diverse demands that ultimately produces 'a people'. The shock of the cold-blooded murder of a 15-year-old by someone who is supposed to protect people had a far-reaching effect: 'You could see all sorts of people, from football fans to immigrants' (Sakis, 30).

This need to symbolically correct Greek society, expressed sometimes in violence, sometimes in more articulated forms of protests, was also the first step of bringing diverse groups of people together. Apart from anarchist and left groups, December 2008 saw the emergence of new political agents: young school children who organised and participated in demonstrations when schools opened the following Monday. The incorporation of other individuals and groups started to suggest a diverse composition which went beyond the usual confines. One participant recalled: 'I saw people from the 80s who don't come out anymore. I saw the young ones [...] But also many people who have nothing to do with that. Neighbours, people who have nothing to do with the left or anything political or revolutionary' (Omega, 46).

In Laclau's populist theory this is described as creating a 'chain' (each link being one group) that establishes a relation of equivalence between what were up to now disassociated groups, ideas or demands. In a way this process is simplifying the social field by creating two sides: those who are part of the chain and those who aren't.[26] Although we started seeing something of this process here (through the recognition that the December events did not just attract the usual suspects but brought in people from different paths of life), we were still observing a very embryonic stage of the process. It was only later, with the Aganaktismenoi (Greek indignants), that this process really started to form a more stable, though not permanent, chain that we can connect with the formation of 'a people'.

From Riots to Populist Movements

We can see this first step towards bringing diverse groups together in the events of December 2008 in Greece (and more so in the 2011 Indignados movements in both Greece and Spain, as I discuss later on). A similar type of proto-articulation was present in protest Occupy movements in Britain and the US, which directly challenged the existing economic and political system in the respective countries and globally. They stopped short of leading to a significant left-populist moment (until recently at least) for reasons I examine later. But it is interesting to ponder for a moment what happened in these countries, since for a long time the crisis was perceived as an Anglo-American issue.

I am referring to the Occupy Wall Street movement, which from September 2011 until mid-November occupied a New York park. It was eventually raided and evicted by the police. It did, however, inspire transnational protests under the 'Occupy' name and it perceived itself as part of the unrest not only in the Western but also in the Arab world, from Egypt to Bahrain. Visual images shared via social media suggest that the participants at Occupy viewed themselves as part of a global wave challenging the authoritarian and liberal democratic political and economic establishments and police brutality. According to Calhoun, this had an important effect in that it inspired protests in different parts of the world but also because it enabled the circulation of tactical ideas.[27]

The British branch, Occupy London, started a month later in October 2011 when a group of activists tried to camp outside the London Stock Exchange but were pushed back by private security and ended up in the space in front of St Paul's Cathedral, with a second camp a bit further away in Finsbury Square. The camps lasted until well into 2012, St Paul's being cleared by authorities in February 2012 and the Finsbury camp, the last one standing, in June 2012. The initial statement (a 'work in progress' according to the principles of direct democracy) stated that the protest was against the bank crisis and the cuts that followed but also more generally against 'global tax injustice'.[28] It described itself as composed of different ethnicities, religions, backgrounds, generations, etc. in an attempt to show the diversity of those who can potentially be part of the movement, and it expressed solidarity with the 'global oppressed'.

Again we see an attempt to form a chain of equivalence, on the one hand bringing together diverse groups of people, and on the other hand creating a clear political division between 'the people' and, in this case, 'the corporations', the name of the enemy in this initial statement. This is what the main motto in both Britain and the US indicated, a division between the 99 per cent ('the people') and the 1 per cent (the corporations, the very wealthy or the 'current system') on the other. Like the Occupy movement in the US, Occupy London adopted direct democracy and its methods for reaching decisions at its General Assembly point to a challenge to the political system that goes beyond strict economism and an aspiration for global democracy.[29]

An interesting expansion in the creation of 'a people' in this case was the role and involvement of the canon of St Paul's Cathedral, Rev. Giles Fraser, in the Occupy London events. Fraser expressed his support by publicly saying he was happy for the protesters to exercise their right to peacefully protest in front of the cathedral, an important early intervention that helped prevent the eviction of the camp in its early days. Soon after he became a voice from inside the Church of England that tried to bring a Christian dimension to the debate, on the side of the protesters. Writing often for the *Guardian*, in November 2011 he argued that 'The Occupy movement is a moment of God-given opportunity to rediscover Christian holiness: not in rich temples, but justice'.[30] Fraser was later moved to a different parish but his involvement is interesting for two reasons. First because his intervention had the potential for expanding the protest into a new group (Christians) in a way that echoes Liberation theology,[31] and second because he later adopted a 'Lexit' position (left exit from the EU) during the Brexit debates. Lexit was adopted by the traditional left and it demonstrates how the generalised economic grievances were articulated in a populist project like Brexit in the UK.

One can see the Occupy movement (in both Britain and the US) as an attempt to create a chain of equivalence that tried to expand beyond national borders, although it did ultimately fail to expand beyond particular sectors within each country. The Occupy movement points to the need to engage with populism not only as a case confined within national borders but also as a transnational process.

Occupy was successful as a transnational bridging process but less so as a national one. In terms of its transnational operation, not only did it enable different national 'branches' to emerge in different countries and attempt to unite diverse 'people' to form 'the 99 per cent', but the participants tried to connect very diverse struggles and contexts together (from Tunisia and Egypt to the US and Europe) and bridge the demands of the West and other parts of the world. The second important feature is that Occupy had explicit tactics of direct democracy (assemblies for decision making) similar to the Indignados movement in Greece and Spain.[32] The question then is why did Occupy fail to get beyond the mainly activist circles and become (to some extent at least) a challenge to neoliberalism and the 'politics as usual' way of doing things? One of the possible explanations offered by scholars (mainly focusing on the US case) is that occupations have 'a tendency to drive a wedge between the protesters and liberals who were sympathetic to many of the mobilisation's messages. They [protesters] created sanitary problems, potential health and safety issues, and traffic problems. They made mayors and university presidents into enforcers of order.'[33] That may have been the case for the Occupy London too (although we saw the opposite, even if limited, dynamic with the Church of England). The only cases we have of fully 'populist' operations at the heart of a movement are the Indignados movements and their occupations of the squares in Greece and Spain.

Another explanation focuses on the inability of the Occupy movement 'to convert electronic communications into the energy and community that derive from face-to-face contact. The outlook for the effectiveness of the movement is decidedly limited unless an alliance of disparate groups develops to press for reforms within the political system.'[34] The first part of the argument regarding electronic communications, while it could be a contributing factor, is quite exaggerated. I agree with Gitlin on the need for face-to-face communication but this could have been something not necessarily related to the movement participants but taken on and brought into the community by other actors, unions, parties and so on. The second part of the argument, however, is much closer to the aims of this book: it refers to the need of moving from one site of resistance (movements/society) to another (electoral politics). Gitlin mentions the 'phobia' of formal organisation and political parties, especially in relation to Occupy.[35] I disagree that the process of bringing disparate groups together is not possible at the actual site of the occupation (as we shall see with the Indignados), but I do believe that a challenge has to cut across sectors of society and ultimately move to the level of formal politics – in contemporary liberal democracies that means electoral politics.[36]

We are now getting to the heart of this book: left populism is not only an electoral strategy, it is a process that starts with movements. That doesn't mean that any movement will entail this dynamic of bringing diverse groups together to create 'a people' that will then lead to an electoral (or other) challenge to the existing political order. Some do, however, which is what makes the Indignados movement in Greece and Spain so important.

The Indignados Movement and the Expansion of Grievances

The protests in Greece and Spain known as the Aganaktismenoi (Greece), the Indignados (Spain) or collectively the Movements of the Squares are of great significance because, much more than any of the protests mentioned earlier, they are closely connected with the development of two left-populist parties: Podemos in Spain and Syriza in Greece. By 2011, when the Indignados mobilisations started, the financial crisis of 2007–8 had become a fully fledged crisis of political representation. The Indignados started to reflect on ways to make political representation more representative of 'the people' rather than the elites. This is what the Indignados and the Occupy movements have in common: the clear separation of 'the people' on the one hand (or the 99 per cent) and the political elites or *la casta* on the other. What changed the game in Greece and Spain is that the movements managed to bring together diverse grievances, classes and groups of people that Occupy didn't. Furthermore, in these countries the energy and dynamism of the movement was later expressed at the electoral level, with two left-leaning parties, Podemos and Syriza, which in their early stages at least represented a genuine populist challenge. (This is not to suggest that countries like the UK and US were immune to populism. Unfortunately, there the creation of 'a people' took a right-wing turn.)

The Movement of the Squares, although different in that it was underpinned by the economic grievances that followed the financial crisis, was similar to the movements of the 1960s in that it could not be interpreted in terms of one-class grievances. In other words, it wasn't a working-class movement organised by the usual working-class agents, for example the KKE in Greece or IU in Spain. The left in these countries was part of the movement, but the movement exceeded it: something bigger was at stake. It is not accidental that in Greece, because the indignant movement did not fit comfortably with traditional working-class politics, the newspaper that attacked it most was not the 'establishment press' but the KKE party newspaper *Rizospastis*. The then leader of the KKE, Aleka Papariga, and others argued that this movement didn't represent a serious challenge to the establishment and a political alternative.[37]

Their take was misleading, since the movement brought people to the streets of Greece who had never demonstrated before and questioned the legitimacy of the political elites. The former leader of the KKE, however, is right in that the movement did not try to seize power, storm parliament or create the type of revolutionary moment that would put an end to capitalism once and for all. After all, the KKE itself had long ago become part of the electoral terrain and, in a way, part of the established political order. The decision of the KKE to call its own separate demonstrations (as it often does) did not help its electoral prospects: it never managed to exceed its usual national electoral share of between 5 and 9 per cent (the lowest was in June 2012 at 4.5 per cent; the highest was in May 2012 at 8.5 per cent).[38]

For those with a different approach, however, the movement did manage to create the conditions for a new electoral challenger to emerge: Syriza. It got into power and, even if it did not manage to deal a more decisive blow to the establishment, nationally and transnationally, we should try to understand the reasons for this.

The Spanish Indignados were launched first on 15 May 2011 (as the anti-austerity movement 15M), and coincidences connected the two movements from the start. One story alleges that when the Spanish Indignados gathered in Puerta del Sol (Madrid), a banner with the sarcastic slogan 'Silence, or we will awake the Greeks' (others say it read 'The Greeks are still sleeping') linked the situation in the two countries and shamed the Greeks for not taking action. This account has been disputed by Greek activists, attributing the alleged banner to a football match incident, while other participants have a different story to tell. An alternative story they recall was how demonstrators in front of the Spanish embassy in Athens met with Greek activists preparing a demonstration at Syntagma on 20 May. They combined forces in Greece and utilised the already active website real-democracy.gr (a platform initiated by the Spanish Indignados at www.democraciareallya.es).[39] One Greek activist recalls the discussion he had with those demonstrating in front of the Spanish embassy in Athens, inviting them to take part in the demonstration under preparation in Athens: 'I suggested they join us at Syntagma Square, this is where the crowds would gather after the Facebook call. They came, 50 people, but they brought real-democracy.gr with them and eventually it was adopted as a central site.'

The links between the Greek and Spanish crisis, resistance and exploration of potential solutions goes beyond the Indignados demonstrations. A feeling of common destiny continued at grassroots level and, later, at the electoral level with Podemos and Syriza, and their respective leaders Pablo Iglesias and Alexis Tsipras. The Indignados/Aganaktismenoi in both countries managed to expand the grievances of the Spanish and Greek people horizontally (the equivalence chain). Íñigo Errejón, number two in Podemos, explains how the 15M movement not only expanded discontent horizontally but also how it politicised certain issues which were previously seen as private grievances. He recalls one particular event in Puerta del Sol when 'people affixed post-it notes written in the first person, notes telling about their particular individual situation', like being stuck at home with their parents and having to hold down several jobs to make ends meet.[40]

Similarly the diversity of demands that moved from the private to the political domain demonstrate the process from isolated individual grievances to the formation of 'a people': 'the indignant pensioner (whose pension has been devalued), the indignant parent … the indignant shop owner (whose clientele is now diminished), the indignant taxpayer (whose reduced salary cannot accommodate the increased rate of taxation)'.[41] The density and the diversity of the protests of the squares were acclaimed by the mainstream media as 'magical', 'a miracle', 'something new'.[42]

These different positions and identities were brought together under the umbrella of indignation with old and new political identities from the 'indignant conservative' to the 'indignant communist' and the 'indignant fascist'.[43] The significance of this diversity is downplayed in other accounts which argue that the Greek mobilisations were mainly composed of 'a broad range of people with protest experience, not just the young or the politically detached' (as in Spain for example). The authors, however, accept that the Indignados/Aganaktismenoi in 2011 saw an expansion of activities as many other scholars have suggested.[44] It is true that part of the Indignados were involved in previous left extraparliamentary and parliamentary groups, but we have to remember that what enabled the expansion of these demonstrations was that none of these groups carried any political identifications during the 2011 protests in Greece. Attempts to set up political stalls with material from particular left organisations were not tolerated. Furthermore, and paradoxically given the horizontalist/autonomist character of the movement, anarchist groups were also excluded due to fear of violence (this does not mean that anarchists were not part of the demos, on the contrary, but not as a bloc).

A survey by the Greek Public Issue agency in June 2011 reported that 35 per cent of the population claimed to have taken part in the Movement of the Squares,[45] and given the media attention this number does not strike me as exaggerated. This diversity meant those who had at some point or another passed through Syntagma or other squares were not from the usual networks of activists, even if some of those may have had a more important organisational role. This diversity was extended to some far-right elements protesting in front of Syntagma Square in Athens, as one of the symbolic divisions of the protesters started to emerge: the division between upper and lower Syntagma Square – the upper expressing their outrage against the political establishment, while in the lower square assemblies were taking place and alternative democratic demands were being explored.

In theoretical terms the Movement of the Squares is important to those who celebrate the multiplicity and horizontality of these movements and as such their non-hierarchical aspiration.[46] The emphasis on the spontaneity of these movements, however, fails to pay attention to the pre-existing formations (existing networks and preceding instances of collective action that I mentioned earlier in this chapter) upon which the indignants relied, not least in organisational knowledge sharing. Movements do not appear from thin air. The traditional Marxist approach, on the other hand, misses the importance of the horizontalist/autonomous character of these movements. Some of us have shown, however, that we can avoid a 'either/or' situation; we see how in all autonomist attempts there are instances of vertical representation, and focus more on how we move from the more horizontal movements to the more vertical politics at electoral level.[47]

All the collective mobilisations discussed here contribute to the later ascendancy of populist parties in the electoral arena. The London riots and the December 2008 and the Occupy movements expanded the existing networks of citizens and gave expression to a generalised discontent. The Indignados brought diverse grievances together, which in this particular conjuncture led to the articulation of 'a people', a people that was aspiring to a different future than neoliberal politics promised. This is the process of articulation I referred to in Chapter 1.

Lessons from the Grassroots: Movements,
Populism and Political Representation

In one of his speeches in July 2015, during the EU–Greece negotiations and just before signing the new memorandum agreement (the lending agreement between Greece and the Troika setting the austerity and structural adjustment rules for the indebted country), the then Prime Minister Alexis Tsipras said that Greece was in the middle of 'an ideological and political battle'.[48] For neoliberalism to be established as the only viable system even as evidence mounted against it, the language that we (as individuals, as voters, as politicians, as the media) use has to be underpinned by the premises of neoliberalism itself. Language is never neutral, it is instead shaped by the environment it appears in, and in turn it moulds social relations, actions and perceptions. This is one of the things Antonio Gramsci taught us in order to understand how hegemony (moral and ideological leadership by the dominant group) is achieved and how it can be fought.

Immediately after the financial crisis many of the mainstream assumptions of neoliberalism that we had all internalised were put into question. The mainstream economic assumptions regarding supply and demand are premised on the idea that markets are natural,

a force external to society that is independent of socio-economic interests and political and ideological contestation.[49] Another neoliberal
assumption is that the relations between individuals, places or institutions are shaped by a competitive drive (rather than collaboration) and
that debt is a moral failing. This is how media correspondents framed
the financial crisis in Europe. Through this frame they managed to
reduce macroeconomics to household economics, and in doing so pass
judgement on countries like Greece and Spain: 'But surely, if you have
borrowed a lot, you have to cut back as we do when we have spent
too much on our credit cards?' This was a common frame throughout
the crisis around different European countries, and was an attempt to
justify austerity policies.

These austerity policies, the national mechanism to deal with debt
and the crisis, passed the painful remedies of the situation on to the
citizens (especially the most vulnerable) rather than the banks, the
financial institutions or the political institutions that failed to predict
or remedy the crisis. As should have been expected, anger and indignation started to mount. The collapse of economic assumptions and
certainties was one of the contributing factors to the feeling of the
ground disappearing beneath your feet which cut across classes. But it
wasn't the only one.

Since the 1990s political scholars had already started to worry about
the relationship between the people and the centres that were supposed
to represent their interests. This broken relationship had manifested
itself in the decline of mass parties. For some, this lack of commitment
to political principles led to the appearance of 'catch-all' parties that
were focused on winning elections. Others called these new or transformed parties 'electoral-professional parties'.[50] This transformation
in parties was the result of an increasing distance between the electorate and those representing them.

We were in the era of what Colin Crouch called the post-democratic
condition: 'politics' had become a game where elected representatives
and elites worked together towards the maximisation of business interests.[51] These technocratic, managerial ways of governance, together
with the financial crisis that exposed the flaws of the system and the
adaptation of austerity policies that took the form of a huge assault
against the very people that governments were there to protect, all
contributed to a generalised feeling of dislocation. This is what drove

the people in the squares of Greece and Spain, full of indignation regarding the political establishment: an existential feeling that what was known had failed them. This is very different from the opposition to austerity policies that was expressed in Britain. It may have been experienced in a similar way for the UK's most vulnerable, but this feeling never reached those who were relatively well off. Even if they had become less well off since the crisis started, most never faced the abysmal unknown that Southern Europe did.

Political theorists like Antonio Gramsci call this an 'organic crisis' while populist theorists like Ernesto Laclau call it 'dislocation'. The famous Gramscian quote describes this crisis as a crisis of authority, 'when the old is dying and the new cannot be born'. Dislocation, although similar, points to the crisis of identities and the severance of their previous political identifications. Effectively we are discussing the loss of legitimacy of the existing political institutions when capitalism is in crisis. This is a key point: it was not only the shock produced by the collapse of financial institutions that were thought of as 'too big to fail', but also the reaction of the political establishment, which rushed to bail them out but imposed austerity on the population at large. There was a realisation, in other words, that technocratic/managerial governance was not representing the people at either the national and transnational level.

Without this total collapse of trust the emergence of 'a people' willing to take the streets, searching for a new democratic alternative as a matter of urgency, is very unlikely. The aspects of financial crisis and the policies of neoliberalism, combined with the severance of the link between politicians and people, go beyond Southern Europe. In countries like Britain, for example, we do not see the same generalised discontent in the streets, but austerity was one cause of the Labour Party taking a different direction under Jeremy Corbyn. 'A people' was trying to emerge in Britain too, but under different conditions which led in a different direction, ultimately resulting in the left of the Labour Party enduring two electoral defeats and the meteoric rise of a right-wing opportunist.

3

Creating a Party for the Twenty-First Century: New Parties, New Structures?

For those aspiring to a democratic, participatory left party that will challenge the conditions of post-democracy, the lessons from the movements that preceded the creation of such parties are important in understanding two things. First, how diverse demands start to come together to form 'a people' – a people that will later be represented by parties at the electoral level. Second, the experience of the movements, and the movement–party relationship, with its potential to direct contemporary parties in a more participatory direction.

The second point is what I want to focus on in this chapter: whether and how the movements preceding the electoral representation of the demands have changed the organisational structures of the parties (and if they have influenced the ideological repertoire of the 'new' parties). Since the financial crisis all three parties I will discuss have entered the electoral arena following different trajectories, but all three of them represented a diversion from establishment politics.

Syriza (a coalition of twelve left-wing organisations established in 2004) and Podemos (a new party formed after the Indignados movement in 2014) both carried the demands of the movements at an electoral level in their respective countries, facing different challenges at the levels of the party, the electoral process and their political identity. In 2015 the UK Labour Party started a transformation under Jeremy Corbyn's leadership, which had its own peculiarities in terms of party organisation and signalled an ideological turn to the left. Labour opened up a discussion on party organisation and the grassroots, not least because of the increase in membership after the election of Jeremy Corbyn as leader.

My aim is to look at the formation of Podemos and the transformation of Syriza into political parties that in different ways and degrees are related to movements. I will analyse their trajectories and key moments in their political transformation, especially attempts to include aspects of 'horizontality' in their organisational practices and their party rhetoric. It is not only Syriza and Podemos, however, that are of interest here. While these two cases have carried the aspiration of the Indignados movement, Labour has carried the aspiration of the British left for a different party. Syriza and Podemos both largely failed to remain faithful to the promise of horizontality, and Labour under the new management of Keir Starmer (the current leader) seems to regress to its old self. Momentarily, however, many active members of Labour demanded structures that, if taken seriously, would promote greater participation. Let me start with the parties associated with the Indignados movement first.

The Indignados Movement and Political Representation

The Indignados movement was the first moment where the necessary conditions of populism started to take shape: the construction of 'a people' through the diverse demands of those who demonstrated in the squares of Greece and Spain. This 'people' stood against the political establishment nationally (the political establishments of Greece and Spain) and transnationally (against the EU political elites). These conditions create the basis for an 'us versus them' dichotomy which reshaped the political space of the two countries, forming a new dividing line in politics for the next few years. This dichotomy would be further articulated by parties and leaders on the left, as we shall see in the following chapters.

Contrary to what some scholars have argued, the formation of 'a people' did not create a homogeneous group, an undifferentiated mass. Different groups still retained their identity and came into the process with demands that were similar but not necessarily the same. These demands started to come together in a chain (with recognisable and separate links) and in the process of collective action started to be represented by a common name ('indignants'). On the other hand, this chain couldn't include everyone. In the process of creating this collectivity, 'a people', some demands or groups would be left out. This is what we mean by the creation of a political frontier in populism. The 'us' which is just about to start forming cannot include everyone. It can aspire to include the '99 per cent' and may claim to represent the 99 per cent, but in reality it connects some grievances that can be represented under the same umbrella. More importantly, if the chain continued to expand endlessly its power would be seriously diminished. Demands have to come together, but equally some have to be excluded in order to form the other side of the frontier – the 'them'.

The common name 'Indignados' signified that despite the diversity of demands and practices within the movement, a common identity was starting to form, an identity carrying demands that could potentially find expression at the electoral level.

At Syntagma Square, in front of the Greek Parliament, the Indignados were divided into two distinct groups: the upper square (where many Greek flags were visible, and which had some conservative and even far-right elements expressing their own rejection of the establishment)[1] and the lower square, where a new political alternative was deliberated in the daily assemblies. Both were angry at the political elites that had subjected them to a lending agreement that was imposing catastrophic austerity; both were angry that their country was to be enslaved to an impossible-to-serve debt. All seemed to agree that the political elites had been 'misrepresenting' them: their affirmation that 'they don't represent us' implied that the current representatives were distorting the will of the people.

The lower part of the square, however, soon began to search for a different type of representation: 'direct' representation. Direct representation is not a new concept and throughout history there have been attempts to institute democratic processes where delegates transfer the decisions taken by the people to other, 'higher' forums. While a delegate is the 'mouthpiece' of the assembly, elected representatives by contrast takes decisions 'in the name of' those they represent.

Delegation and participatory structures to enable first the participation of the people opposing the establishment and later to reform national democratic structures has a long history and it is part of the European historical imaginary. In a way the Greek and Spanish assemblies became something like the demand for a 'convention'. Whether as gatherings for the English parliaments summoned without the royal prerogative, or associated with the French revolution, or even as a demand from English Jacobins in the late eighteenth and early nineteenth centuries, the name 'convention' points to the popular demand for the reform of parliament. And the starting point is always instituting a different form of representation (like delegation) in the very proceedings that demand democratic reform of the nation state. This is what was at play at the squares: the institution of better forms of representation among those participating, which in turn should be carried to new political actors who then take the demands to the electoral level aiming to reform national (and international) institutions.

Syriza and Podemos tried to institute a different type of organisation as a response to the failure of the previous parties to represent the demands of the period. The demand for 'dignity', which was expressed in the Indignados, was not a demand for recognition as a particular group but had a universalising aspect, enabling the creation of an egalitarian space of inclusion in general.[2] The demand for inclusion would be carried to the party, to the electorate and ultimately to legislative outcomes.

In Spain, in order to enhance democratic participation, those talking at the local assemblies were instructed to avoid speaking in the name of others and when these assemblies sent representatives to the central fora they were again instructed to do so in the most faithful manner possible. Having two representatives per assembly in the process was also an attempt to minimise the abuse of their position.[3] Thus they acted as delegates, mouthpieces for the assemblies, rather than as 'representatives' as we understand them in contemporary liberal democracies (with autonomy to decide themselves on the best course of action).

In the debates around the Indignados movement and contemporary parties, this potentially less distorted representation is understood as 'horizontality'. Despite all efforts, however, horizontality is never fully achieved: no matter how hard we try, some residue of hierarchy remains. And despite the fact that the Indignados movement was decentralised, with dozens of assemblies in cities, towns and even neighbourhoods taking place in both Greece and Spain, the assemblies of Syntagma Square and Puerta del Sol became the privileged, central sites.

There is a process of representation here too, if we think about it in a more abstract way. Syntagma and Sol were not just one node in the network of resistance, but came to 'stand for' the movement: in the media, in the public imaginary, these two squares stood for the movement as a whole. It seems that in the process of representation there is always some 'verticality', so some people or places are more central and privileged than others. The experience of the assemblies testifies to that. We can all come together as equals but the ones who have more experience, who are better at public speaking for example, are more dominant, more 'present' in these democratic exercises.[4]

The million dollar question of course is what happens after the end of the movements. What remains from the assemblies, from the discussions trying to find more direct forms of democracy (even if only as an ideal to strive for), from the novel experience of the participants? What happens as parties take on the demands of these movements and bring them to the electoral level? Do they take any notice of the explicit demand for a different democracy and the implicit one for a more participatory future? Are these parties going to challenge the 'establishment' by instituting more democratic structures internally? Will they become 'parties of the movements',[5] or (as they are labelled in academic debates) 'movement parties'? Did Podemos (as a new party directly connected with the experience of the movements) or Syriza (as an older left formation that took it upon itself to represent the demands of the indignants at an electoral level) learn something in their relationship with these laboratories of political representation? The leadership of Jeremy Corbyn posed a similar question for Labour: would the election of a left leader give voice to the members and make the structures of the party more democratic?

The answers are closely related to the parties' ideological reservoirs and historical precedent on the one hand and to the demands placed on them by the particular political conjuncture on the other. The latter in some cases enabled, in others restricted, the new political party structures and their engagement with electoral politics.

Movement Parties, Members and Technology

The relationship between movements and parties – and the rhetoric of parties about their close relationship – does not mask the fact that we are talking about different forms of presenting demands and taking action. In the past, labour movements were part of the origin of socialist and social democratic parties, but these older labour movements concentrated on demands directed towards the state, such as redistribution of wealth and extension of citizens' rights. These types of demands were part of the Indignados movement, no doubt, but not only. The Indignados movement had also similarities with social movements of the type that emerged from the 1960s onwards. These movements had somewhat different demands: demands not necessarily directed towards the state, but for social and cultural change more broadly. One does not necessarily exclude the other, as some scholars have argued,[6] but we must recognise that the Indignados movement itself was not limited to strictly 'labour' demands but rather representation as such.

The parties that in the past seemed to strive harder for a more 'representative' or horizontal representation were the Western Green parties from the 1970s onwards. Being more representative internally, they gained the labels 'left-libertarian' or 'movement parties'.[7] In practice this was achieved by rotating leaders or spokespersons, by enabling the participation of their members in decision-making processes, by being autonomous from the state and by moving beyond strictly economic demands, for instance challenging state bureaucracy.[8]

The same can be said for the parties associated with the 2008 financial crisis. They responded to the crisis of representation in the post-democratic period that came to its zenith with the financial crisis: it is not only that it became clear that the financial system was flawed and that states were going to make the people to pay for its failure, but also that those who were supposed to represent the people had little interest in their demands and grievances.

The parties that took up the baton from the anti-austerity movement (we can use the term 'movement parties') aspired, or at least seemed to aspire, towards a more horizontal, participatory structure as they brought the socio-economic demands of the movements to the electoral level. This is important: they were not only making economic demands, they were interested in a new way of doing politics, and a new way of bringing the people into politics, that exceeded the usual limits of liberal democratic processes. The tensions created, and ultimately their inability to drastically change the way parties operate, can teach us a lot about the party of the twenty-first century.

In electoral terms the most successful of these parties was Syriza, which formed a coalition government with ANEL[9] that came to power in January 2015 and then was re-elected in September 2015 (after signing a lending agreement with the Troika). Paradoxically, after four and a half years in power and after the elections of Autumn 2019, Syriza launched a new platform, iSYRIZA.gr. Under the slogan 'take Syriza in your hands', it promises to become a tool that will enable members and sympathisers to participate in decision making and to be informed about what is going on in Syriza. The move came after a call by Tsipras on the night of the 2019 election (and by Syriza's political bureau later) for the creation of a mass left party assisted by the potential of digital technologies. This move was part of a more general campaign aiming to increase the number of party members. The new platform's aims were 'to keep you informed according to your individual interests, enable participation in consultation processes and to host a number of other activities'.[10] Despite the promise it still seemed mostly concerned with older forms of information distribution, for example a newsletter which (like the newspapers of a different time) would give information on the operations of Syriza.

The use of new platforms came after a long period in government during which the party had become secondary to the whole process of governing, and the remnants of it together with those who remained in the party had been inactive. The local organisations (the grassroots of the party), mainly charged with supporting governmental policy, were quite inactive and, according to a party officer, this was reflected in the almost total absence of power at the local level.

Numerous times I brought the issue up in public forums[11] (once at an LSE event addressing a Syriza Minister in 2018) and private discussions, and I was always given the same answer: the Syriza government needed people for the state machine, so all the 'manpower [sic]' was absorbed there. As a result the party was not functioning – from the moment Syriza got into power any grassroots activity went out of the window. Only after the 2019 election did the role of the party, and the need for participatory structures within the party, come to the forefront – and even then it was not clear whether that signified a serious shift or just a sound bite to attract new voters.

The tension between Syriza and many party activists, however, had started much earlier. For some it was the signing of the memorandum in July 2015, which led part of the traditional (and potentially more Eurosceptic) left to split from the party. For these groups, while their position was not necessarily homogeneous, a confrontation with the Troika could either lead to the Troika back-pedalling (unlikely) or the withdrawal of Greece from the eurozone or even the EU. Their rationale, not dissimilar to the left groups that supported an exit from the EU during and after the British referendum, was that even if there was economic chaos in the short term, in the long run Greece could prosper with a left government outside the confines of the eurozone.

Beyond these groups, however, many Syriza activists objected to the transformation of Syriza into a party of government with centralised structures, allowing no space for democratic decision-making processes. As one of the activists said:

> I didn't leave the party so much because of the huge disappointment of signing the memorandum [...] I left because it [the signing of the memorandum] was never discussed. It could have been discussed in an emergency conference and we may have lost the vote, but I wouldn't have left because my position lost. I would have had my battle. But they didn't even allow us to have this battle within the party – this is the reason I left.

The lack of democracy, and the inability of Syriza to engage with its own activists/members once in government, was one of the reasons that many disengaged from Syriza. Worse, these groups were left without a political 'home'. While those with a different ideological vision of Syriza continued to operate in their own organisations (from then onwards strongly criticising Syriza in government), those disillusioned with the decision-making process of the party were left with no place to house their political aspirations:

> I did not join anything else. There is nothing else to express me. And the attempts that happened afterwards, although I haven't followed them closely, I only went to one meeting, and they mainly operated with an anti-Syriza fury, concentrating on how they would attack Syriza, which I am not interested in. I am interested in how we will rebuild the left and how these ideas we believe in can find expression in society.

What Syriza was trying to imitate in 2019, after it lost the election, was the Podemos experiments with digital technologies that led to what has been branded 'technopopulism': the enhancement of party membership via digital channels and reliance on digital technologies for participation in decision-making processes. In the case of Podemos we now know that, although the potentials of digital technologies brought a whole new wave of members into the party, members remained relatively passive spectators regarding the power struggles within the party, and often did not get involved in grassroots activity.[12] It is true, however, that the possibilities opened by digital technologies enabled increased participation, and for a time this was one of the priorities of Podemos. The promises of the digital platforms and the new politics were for a while closely connected.

According to a Podemos member who reached the highest ranks of the party, this priority changed in 2016:

> At the beginning Podemos was about a new ethics of politics. To do politics differently. Doing ordinary stuff differently. People were upset about political parties in general. But [...] there was a ceiling for that. In 2016 there was much more about Catalonia, it was about policies, it was much more about the economy [...] 2016 was the end of this ethics of politics, participation, openness, transparency period, let's say.

Both Syriza and Podemos seemed to undergo a similar shift. One can detect different periods in their development: a first period when the participatory structures of the movements and their implementation at party level was a concern of the party, and then a second period when both parties were absorbed by the demands of governing (or aspiring to).

A final note on the new technologies, which is sometimes missed. It is important to recognise the risks embedded in these technologies: the creation of records with sensitive information that cannot be easily deleted (think old posts and tweets) or even databases of political activity that could easily be shared with state agencies. Most importantly, however, optimism about the 'new politics' enabled by technology should be moderated. Without a conscious effort and determination to create new political structures that promote transparency, participation and collaboration these approaches can end up 'proposing the usual things with the tools of tomorrow'.[13]

Finally, there is what it is often called the 'digital divide'. Despite the much wider penetration of new technologies in Western societies, not everyone has the same relationship with them. This is determined particularly by generation, but also gender, economic capacity and other factors. The use of new technologies and, more generally, the extent of the movements' influence on these parties is of course determined by the historical legacy of each party – and we should not forget that Syriza and Podemos had very different historical developments, irrespective of the use of technology. Podemos, although not simply the party of the Indignados movement, is nevertheless the natural continuation of what happened in the Spanish squares. Syriza on the other hand, despite being a new experiment for the left, carried with it many of the centralised structures of previous left organisations.

New Organisational Structures and Old Impediments

Podemos, coming out of the wave of mobilisations I described earlier as the Indignados movement, was keen to create a different type of political party, closer to the horizontalist aspirations of the movements that proceeded it, enabling the organic participation of the membership in decision-making processes. In reality it incorporated the activists of the 15M movement alongside parts of the fragmented traditional left (Izquierda Anticapitalista) and young intellectuals. The three key figures were political scientists at the Universidad Complutense in Madrid: Pablo Iglesias (the general secretary), Íñigo Errejón (later representing the more 'populist' faction in Podemos) and Juan Carlos Monedero (who resigned in April 2015).

It was clear that the differences between these groups would create tensions. As some Podemos figures narrate, there was a discussion in 2015 about whether one had to go to the traditional left and the unions in order to attract people with particular skill sets, or rather invite people from civil society willing to do things differently and train them in a new politics that would fulfil the Podemos aim: to bridge the movement with the party in a new organisational structure. Although it still had some of the traditional organisational elements of left parties, it did promise more participation. Out of the three parties I discuss in this book (Syriza, Podemos and the Labour Party), Podemos is probably the closest to the definition of a movement party, at least in the beginning. According to scholars of movement parties, we can summarise their characteristics as a strong participatory vision, tensions between strategies in the streets and strategies inside political institutions and the attempt to create new subjectivities.[14] Although, as we will see later, the strategic tensions between streets and institutions is prominent to all of them, Podemos was from the start more conscious in terms of creating participatory structures and new subjectivities. The latter can be understood in terms of populism, creating 'a people' (rather than the more traditional left-wing identification based on class), but also in terms of taking on a new political identity by participating in a different type of politics (horizontalist and participatory).

Key in fulfilling the participatory objective of Podemos were the *circulos* (circles), the main grassroots organisational units. Anyone could start one without being registered or being a member and afterwards they could apply for 'validation'. The circles were either geographical (territorial circles) or thematic (sectoral circles) in a particular policy area or professional category, and they had to abide by the documents approved by the citizens' assembly.[15] Citizens' open primaries elect the general secretary, who presides over the citizens' council (the executive organ) and the members of the citizens' council itself. A further commission of democratic guarantees, also elected at open citizens' primaries, is charged with safeguarding the fundamental principles of Podemos.

The organisational structures of the party are not strikingly different from other democratic parties, although the naming of the organs points to the aspiration for direct democracy and popular sovereignty. Rather than having a representational system based on delegation (even if it is more democratic in that delegates transfer the will of the people who elected them more closely than other representatives), the citizens' assembly enables all members and supporters to participate and vote for the leader and the political organs of Podemos. This was the true innovation. Rather than following the membership system of the traditional parties, everyone – that is, all who are interested in the politics of Podemos, not only the members – could elect the general secretary, the citizens' council and the parliamentary candidates in open primaries.

However, the circles did not retain their initial role in shaping the party. They were gradually deactivated, the result of the party facing a strategic dilemma of operating at the electoral level: should they focus on gaining centrist voters or continue with social mobilisation? As the balance tilted towards the first, centralising tendencies became more prominent.[16]

Back in 2014 Podemos activists I spoke to were aware of the issues around the participatory promises, but were also hopeful. One of them said:

> The guarantee is the people. We are watching them. I don't know how participatory we will be in the future. They can say you can do this and that but who knows, maybe they can do what they want the next day. But here we are and I do believe that the leaders, like Pablo Iglesias, are passionate about these issues.

Podemos launched their internet campaign in 2014 and within the first 20 days had 100,000 members. Registration did not involve the usual financial contribution required by other parties, and within days Podemos had become the third largest party in Spain, behind the PP (right wing) and PSOE (social democrats). Registration allowed members to vote at the first Podemos citizens' assembly, named 'Sí, Se Puede' (Yes We Can)[17] or Vistalegre I, and to participate in the discussion forums held on Podemos internet platforms such as Plaza Podemos.[18]

During the first citizens' assembly in 2014, Iglesias proposed alliances between Podemos and other parties and organisations including the *mareas*[19] and En Comú.[20] This opening to other anti-establishment forces was in accordance with the focus of Vistalegre I, which effectively saw Podemos as an electoral machine ready to establish its newly founded power in municipal, regional and national elections. Even Juan Carlos Monedero,[21] who was emphasising the importance of social mobilisation, was at that stage not hostile to an electoral focus. Juan Carlos Monedero, Teresa Rodriguez[22] and Pablo Echenique[23] had all argued during Vistalegre for more participatory structures that would make the party more horizontalist and plural. The power of the general secretary (Pablo Iglesias since 2014) was another point of contention,[24] which in terms of populist theory supports the critique of populism around the issue of verticality enacted by a strong (charismatic) leader. This critique has been associated both with right-wing populist leaders like Trump and with left-populist leaders like Chávez. Chávez's case has to be examined within the South American context, and many commentators have simultaneously praised his leadership as a corrective to the broken politics of the country while criticising the tendency of his administration towards corruption, patronage and clientelism.[25] The leaders of left populism in Europe are not authoritarian but, as is the case with some of the parties I discuss here, do preserve the more hierarchical ways of doing party politics despite their participatory promises.

At the Podemos citizens' assembly, as is often the case, the documents put to a vote by those registered had been prepared in advance by a team of 26 (coordinated by the university professor Luis Alegre) rather than collectively, in the first place. On the one hand, having the people/members deciding on the organisational structure, ethics and political direction of a party is a huge step towards horizontality. On the other hand, the manner in which the vote was organised raised a lot of questions. From many proposals put forward, the ones dominating were Pablo Iglesias' 'Claro Que Podemos' and 'Sumando Podemos' by Pablo Echenique, the main rival of Iglesias during this time. It is the latter who suggested a three-way leadership, which would allow more plurality at the top and differentiate the party from the traditional ones. The broad powers invested in the general secretary make him not only more powerful in traditional terms but also more visible in media terms and reinforces a 'leader' culture. For some, the first citizens' assembly established the basis for a vertical party, loosely connected with its own base. Its supporters justified this as an 'exception' due to the economic and political crisis.[26]

One Podemos activist told me that the turning point for Podemos was 31 May 2015, when they propsed a massive demonstration in Madrid called 'March for Change'. Iglesias pronounced this a 'new cycle': from that moment Podemos was to be an 'electoral machine' trying to gain institutional power, at the expense of the 'movement' side of the party which believed in the need for wider social change from below.[27]

By the second party conference, Vistalegre II, which took place in Madrid in February 2017, the power dynamics had changed. One of the notable differences was that Pablo Iglesias' challengers were no longer the 'anti-capitalist' group but now the 'populist' Errejonistas (led by Íñigo Errejón) who wanted to 'mainstream' the party,[28] in other words making it attractive to diverse groups of voters, and Miguel Urbán. Iglesias emerged victorious with 51 per cent of the votes against 34 per cent for Errejón and 13 per cent for Urbán. In light of the 2016 general election, and despite the previous discourse which emphasised the differences between Podemos and the 'old left' (not to mention the attempt to bypass the left–right dichotomy, which I will return to later), Podemos formed an electoral alliance with IU and others and became Unidas Podemos,[29] thus taking a left turn.

At Vistalegre II, Teresa Rodríguez, Pablo Echenique and other previous rebels stood now with the leader. Errejón and Iglesias agreed about the need to end vertical structures, decentralise the party and give voice to minorities,[30] although this did not prevent the unavoidable split between Iglesias and Errejón.

In terms of the organisational structures of the party, the difference between the first and second citizens' assembly was beautifully explained by some striking visuals: the hand waving, a gesture coming from the 15M movement and grounding the party in the movement tradition, had now been replaced by raised fists (for Iglesias supporters) and the victory sign (for Errejón's supporters).

The promise of more horizontal participation at party level was supposed to be mediated by technology, but instead we ended up with a version of 'audience democracy',[31] with an emphasis on the person of the leader rather than the party. Podemos, as a new party with more flexible structures of organisation (the *circulos*), promised to create a different relationship with its membership and sympathisers using electronic platforms. Without doubt, digital networks have been important for making Podemos a mass party; however, those engaged in digital participation are not necessarily party militants who operate at the grassroots level but only minimally involved via the digital platforms. As a result the experiment ended in an unevenness between the activism of those in the circles and the much bigger group of less committed sympathisers.

Furthermore, decision-making processes through digital platforms are as open to top-down manipulation as the older forms of decision making, especially when the group entrusted with the operation of the digital platforms is close to the leadership and it is possible to win top party positions through media visibility (including both traditional media and social media).[32]

Although the creation of Podemos was indebted to the movement that proceeded it (15M), as Errejón admits, the creation of the party was an initiative of activists and citizens with no previous consultation either with 15M or the indignants.[33] Podemos as a party had to create not only its organisational structures but also its ideological orientation from nothing. In terms of organisation, we saw the tension between the aspiration to creating a movement party (at least at the beginning) and the progressive domination of more vertical structures. Furthermore, this verticality tended to depend on the central figure of the leader rather than on party structures as a whole. As a result the whole experiment was characterised by the antagonistic visions of the different key figures – and especially the two most prominent ones, Íñigo Errejón and Pablo Iglesias – rather than on wide and active participation:

> The circulos didn't work. It was a mixture of things that came from the Indignados movement [...] it was the mixture of the old local praxis of a traditional party, it was very Indignados oriented, it was very open, very digital, very online, very much about discussing online, a digital public sphere, this is what Podemos brought to the table. This didn't work. To be honest part of the membership was very old, there was a huge gap between the leadership and the membership. The membership was much older and old school. The leadership was younger and was divided in two sides between the more traditional and the more state of the art, let's say.

Ideological Repertoire and the Left–Right Divide

The organisational and ideological form of the 'new', left-populist parties like Syriza and Podemos was also dependent on their positioning of the left–right divide, which emerged from their histories as well as the particular political situation in each country. Podemos, according to Pablo Iglesias, was keen to reshape the political map of the country. He said: 'They wanted us to play on a board where everything was sold, where the cards are dealt, and we said no, what we want is to be at the centre of the board: there is a social majority of the country that demands decency.'[34]

At that point he meant that the new party, Podemos, was the one that had to set the rules of the game, forcing the rest of the parties to position themselves around him and not the other way around. This is what is called 'transversality': trying to set the rules of the game, avoiding being branded according to the categories of the existing political order, and effectively creating 'a people' that goes beyond left and right. In terms of how this approach could bridge the diverse demands of the squares, it has been argued that

> Those who demand better salaries cannot be seen as different from those who want the oceans without plastics: a transformative force must bring them together in the struggle for equality, because both demands go against market productivity. This is transversality, which constitutes the path for any progressive struggle.[35]

I return to this in Chapter 6, in relation to Brexit. What is important in terms of how Podemos was shaped organisationally is that when this approach was abandoned the older forms of doing politics again became influential within Podemos. The form this took is the shift towards an alliance with IU, which resulted in the coalition of Unidas Podemos (United We Can). This move was resisted by Íñigo Errejón and those more inclined to his position, a position very much marked by his interest in left populism. Errejón was categorically against the further merging of the two parties, but in 2016 the relationship between Podemos and IU was putting the influence of traditionally left parties like IU firmly back in the map and, in a way, pushing Podemos further from its origins.[36]

Back in 2015 IU and Podemos were antagonists. When Tsipras invited Pablo Iglesias to join him on stage at a big public talk in Athens back in 2015 Cayo Lara (representing IU) was fuming. Next to him was the president of the UK Greece Solidarity Campaign (and general secretary of the TSSA union), Manuel Cortes, who overheard him saying in Spanish that he couldn't believe Tsipras was sharing the stage with Iglesias after IU had supported Syriza from the start. For Podemos in 2015, IU was part of the old political establishment and the left–right divide had to be transversed.

And yet, in cases such as Syriza, although the cohabitation with the traditional left proved impossible within the party, an alliance between left parties enabling accession to power would have been the first choice in 2015.

Although there are many similarities between the socio-political context of Greece and Spain, not least the shared legacy of the respective dictatorships, the differences are equally striking when it comes to the 'organisational vibe' of Syriza and Podemos. In 2014–15, being a member of Syriza and working closely with some of the Podemos activists in London, I used the following image to describe the difference: whenever I entered a room with Podemos activists, whether they knew me or not, they were coming to me with open arms and we were hugging (hugging and kissing when you greet someone is common in both Greece and Spain). This never happened with most of my Syriza comrades, neither in London nor in Greece. What was greeting me was suspicion: 'who is she?', 'why is she representing Syriza?', 'which organisation [of Syriza] does she come from?' It could have been personal antipathy to me, but I think there was something else there: to a much larger extent than Podemos, Syriza had and I believe still has the qualities that characterise the hierarchical, 'old' left instead of the vibrant, more open and horizontalist movements. The tension between traditional left structures, with centralism and verticality, and new devolved and more horizontalist practices inspired by the squares is again evident. As one Syriza member said:

> Syriza had and still has an organisational structure which is old fashioned: with the hierarchies, the political bureau, the central committee … but what changed with the squares in Syriza is that it learned what it means to have an assembly. Suddenly Syriza learned how to have local assemblies, open, not the traditional, closed meetings that were happening at the offices of the local party among members. The Movement of the Squares moved to the neighbourhoods and held meetings. This was done by the organised left, not the indignant in general […] another thing is that it [Movement of the Squares] radicalised the youth, which changed its structures a

bit. The Syriza youth at that point wasn't yet unified – there was still the Synaspismos Youth, which had its own structures, but there was also the Syriza youth which had an informal committee, one person from each organisation of Syriza, but we could decide very few things because we didn't have a structure. The Squares enabled us to do more things, some small festivals, we wrote some announcements [as Syriza youth] which before we couldn't do within Syriza. Also, Syriza became more mature, moved away from the logic of the separate organisations and it did become a unified Syriza. This maturity came with the Squares.

Syriza of course has been (at least on paper) sympathetic to social movements, some organisations and tendencies more than others, and the Greek indignant movement was composed not only of people that engaged in collective action for the first time but also of seasoned activists, including members of Syriza or one of the organisations that initially came together to form Syriza. Many of them had been actively engaged with the European Social Forum and had been part of the anti-globalisation movement and student movement, more recent campaigns and so on.

Going back to the 1960s and 1970s, while in many North European countries we saw a proliferation of movements for gender equality, civil rights and anti-nuclear and anti-war protests, the European South was facing dictatorial regimes and student uprisings (as in the case of Greece) were primarily popular uprisings against the dictatorship. The dictatorship had slowed down the popular radicalisation and youth rebellion, and the popular uprising in Greece was the Polytechnic uprising in 1973.

As in other parts of Europe, the movements of the 1960s were met with suspicion or at least hesitation by the communist parties, and part of the left never totally overcame this suspicion. In the late 1960s the Greek Communist Party (along with many others) was going through seismic reconfigurations that followed the Prague Spring, which led to the split of the party into KKE (orthodox) and KKE internal (the Eurocommunist tradition). And yet, even the latter did not fully embrace the uprising at the start. Ultimately both communist parties became part of the uprising, but the suspicion towards certain groups within it did not go away.[37] Animosities with Trotskyist and other groups continued, and one of the important organisational contributions of Syriza decades later was that it brought all of these part of the left together (with the exception of the KKE).

Syriza was set up as a coalition of the left party Synaspismos (SYN) and twelve other organisations in 2004. It was shaped by four tendencies: (1) the EDA[38]-KKE tradition (and the tension between Eurocommunism versus pro-Soviet communism); (2) the extraparliamentary left (including diverse groups like Trotskyites and Maoists); (3) the tradition of the alter-globalisation movement of the 2000s; and (4) the social democratic tradition, incorporated into Syriza mainly after the 2012 election.[39]

The largest party in the Syriza coalition, SYN (Coalition of the Left, of Movements and Ecology) was already strongly oriented towards creating links with the movements. For SYN the role of the left 'is not to guide but to participate in movements and try to influence them, while learning from them'.[40] The relationship with the movements – national and transnational – was explicit right from the 2013 Founding Congress. In the Syriza conference manifesto (Political Decision Plan) it is stated that:

> SYRIZA is coordinated with the social movements and the popular demands [...]. The Left government will come as the outcome of this huge popular movement and initiative. The experience of the first, magnificent anti-memorandum fight of the big demonstrations and the squares and the slowing down of the movement that followed showed us that the fight for the defeat of the memorandum governments will take longer.[41]

In this spirit of coordination between the movements and social demands, Syriza funded (partly through a 'solidarity deduction' of the Syriza MPs' salary) the creation of the umbrella organisation Solidarity4All in 2013. The aim of the organisation has since been to link the different autonomous solidarity groups operating in Greece into a network enabling the exchange of knowledge, information and simultaneously increasing their online and offline visibility. I return to these solidarity networks later on because their contribution in proposing new ways of organising economic production was one of the most interesting aspects of social experimentation during and after the crisis.

To signal a transformative process from a small left party to a broader organisation able to incorporate diverse social groups and demands, Syriza was symbolically inaugurated with the addition of the acronym EKM (United Social Front) to the party's name. The displacement of the people's demands from the movement of Aganaktismenoi to Syriza had been decisive for the identity of the party and for a potential electoral victory. Nevertheless, Syriza as a party was progressively losing its ability to sustain grassroots activity.

As a coalition of different left-wing organisations and activists, Syriza had a number of organisational characteristics that were about to change as electoral victory started to come within reach. As a coalition the constituent organisations of Syriza had retained their autonomy in terms of internal organisation, political direction and public activity, and had an established a role in the decision-making process of the Syriza coalition as a whole. This was about to change with the announcement by Alexis Tsipras of the self-dissolution of Synaspismos, and an invitation to the rest of the Syriza organisations to do the same. These tensions became apparent at the first founding conference of Syriza as a unified party. The conference (10–14 July 2013), attended by some 3,500 delegates elected by the local members' organisations, was marked by intense reactions to the proposal of self-dissolution of the different organisations. A compromise was agreed, giving 'reasonable' time to the organisations to dissolve or to cease their public presence. Instead, party members were encouraged to join tendencies, promoting collective positions within the party and publicly, as long as they specified that they did not express the official position of the party.

For some this was a necessary step dictated by Greek electoral law, which offers a bonus of 50 seats to the party that comes first in the national elections. For others the new structure of Syriza assisted in the development of a more leader-centric orientation within the party. But these organisational decisions were not the only ones responsible for Syriza losing touch with its own grassroots and activists. As in the case of Podemos, as power came within its grasp more 'pragmatic' decisions were made, and these decisions were made centrally. One activist, who was part of one of the committees working on the Syriza programme, remembers:

We created a programme that was never used [...] This is when the game was lost, before the signing of the memorandum, at the elections of 2015 when they [the leadership] turned their back on the work that had been done the previous years and instead focused on a 'realistic' programme. The 'realistic' programme for the leadership was, in my opinion, only related to the economic side of things, unemployment, labour market, etc., there were no other issues – for example the refugee crisis, the environment, foreign policy, etc.

The Labour Party and the Transformation of 'Old' Party Structures and Ideas

In the UK we find a different political trajectory from the squares to electoral and party politics. In 2011 two protest movements reacted to the disenfranchisement of communities and questioned the legitimacy of the political system: the London riots in August 2011, and Occupy London from September 2011 onwards. The student protests in November–December 2010 also helped the radicalisation of a younger generation. None of these protests, however, managed to bring together diverse demands extending discontent across different sectors of the population.

In the case of the London riots, the looting and violence and the absence of clear demands obscured the root causes of the events and the anger accumulated in communities that had been victimised, marginalised and excluded from the benefits of globalisation for decades. The Occupy movement failed to generate a widespread response that would transform electoral politics. Many commentators try to present the period before the election of Jeremy Corbyn as leader of the Labour Party as the period of a widespread anti-austerity movement, and although it is true that there were anti-austerity protests and at least a nationwide one in 2015, it did not have the same duration, nor did it reach the numbers nor the diverse social strata, that it did in Greece and Spain. One possible contributing factor is that the financial crisis had not produced the same dislocatory effect on the British working and middle classes, and as such they still identified with the institutions – including the political parties – of the existing economic and political system.

Instead the 'movement' that promised to challenge electoral politics in Britain was Corbynism, via Momentum: the organisation built out of Jeremy Corbyn's campaign for the leadership of the Labour Party in 2015.[42] The campaign to elect Jeremy Corbyn did manage to unite different parts of the parliamentary (Labour Party) and non-parliamentary left, including groups such as Left Unity. Momentum defines itself as 'a people-powered, vibrant movement. We aim to transform the Labour Party, our communities and Britain in the interests of the many, not the few.'[43]

As one of the organisers of the campaign said:

Momentum emerged after the first leadership election, after Jeremy Corbyn became the leader of the Labour Party [...] a number of predominantly young people who had come together to campaign for him. He was elected but he needed support within the Labour Party, so Momentum was a machine to support him within the Labour Party. At that point no one had expected him to win and there was a lot of hostility against him, particularly from members of parliament. [...] It started with no structure, just people came together: a combination of some old 'heads', people who had been a long time around campaigning for democracy in the Labour Party using the enthusiasm of this huge force that wanted to change the Labour Party. But now it is much more democratic: In order to join it you have to be a member of the Labour Party [...] unions can affiliate and send delegates [...] now it looks more like any other Labour Party structure.

The creation of Momentum was the outcome of organisational changes by the previous Labour leader Ed Miliband, which enabled the party to shift to the left. By instituting a system of one member, one vote, Miliband shifted power from the Parliamentary Labour Party (members of parliament) and the unions towards ordinary members.[44] The additional inclusion of 'registered supporters' in the 2015 leadership contest only reinforced this. Limiting the power of the Parliamentary Labour Party had the effect of making the party more horizontal in its structure. Being able to register as a 'supporter'

for a small fee gave a whole new constituency the ability to participate in the leadership election. The modest shift in the organisational
structure thus went hand in hand with changes to the party's base of
members, supporters and voters. After Corbyn became leader of the
Labour Party in 2015, Momentum became the agent of further calls
for a potentially more horizontalist representation of members. One
of these was the call for an easier 'deselection' process of sitting MPs
and a more open and inclusive selection process, allowing members
to choose their preferred candidates before each election instead of
the current MP becoming the candidate automatically. According to
Momentum, opening up the selection process from the start would
bring MPs closer to their members and their communities.[45]

Yet most of the organisational changes during the period of Corbyn's
leadership were limited. According to one high-ranking officer:

> We had democratic structures, but they were ignored. You didn't
> have to change the structures, you just needed a leadership that
> would abide by the democratic decisions [...] the only democratic
> change was on deselection and the number of seats on the National
> Executive that are directly elected by members. You have seats for
> the unions and seats for the CLPs [party branches]. There were
> only six CLP seats. That has now increased to nine.

From its inception, Momentum itself was not as inclusive and open
as a social movement (although at the beginning it was more open
in terms of the membership and future direction). Like other organisations inside Labour it has a particular identity as a pressure group:
rather than simply being an agent of change, it aims to engage supporters who are sympathetic to Corbyn's message and promote left
politics within the party.

This is reflected in the current organisational structures of
Momentum. Since adopting its new constitution in 2017, Momentum
requires all new members to be Labour Party members. Furthermore,
the organisation was split from the start between those who prefer
the traditional branch-based structure (seen as more susceptible to
'entryism' by non-Labour groups) and those who prefer a more 'virtual'
structure (empowered by digital platforms) that is more attractive
to younger activists but also more easily controlled by the organisa-

tion's founder, Jon Lansman.[46] In its current form the key decisions are taken by the National Coordinating Group, made up of members of the three geographical divisions, Labour public officers, members nominated by the affiliated trade unions and members of other affiliated organisations. The organisation has a digital platform, 'My Momentum', and voting takes place online.

The tensions between horizontality and verticality are also evident in a number of power struggles between the membership and the Labour leadership. One such case happened during the 2017 Labour Conference, when a Momentum email to its supporters urged delegates to vote to prioritise the discussion on issues such as housing and the NHS at the party conference rather than Brexit. As a result, Brexit was not among the eight priority issues debated at the conference, saving Corbyn from confronting this divisive issue. This testifies to a vertical structure where the Momentum membership is supposed to follow the line decided by its leadership – a leadership whose primary aim is to support the Labour Party leadership of Corbyn.

To be fair, structures enabling democratic participation within the Labour Party, while somewhat hierarchical, were always present. It is just that the democratic processes were rarely listened to by previous Labour leaderships. The way the Labour Party allows its grassroots to participate in decision-making processes is clear:

> If the branch passed your policy, then you send it to your CLP, if the CLP agrees it is send to the party conference. [...] When you go to conference (every CLP is entitled to send motions to conference) 20 topics are chosen for discussion. Provided your motion is one of those topics it gets debated and voted upon. What happens usually is that they debate the most topical issues.

Obviously this process can be manipulated, and it has been manipulated in the past in many ways. Potentially, however, it could enable high levels of participation.

Lessons in Terms of the Organisational Structures of Contemporary Parties

The tension between movement and party remains unsolved in all the cases we have looked at, despite their influence and relationship with the movements. Despite the desire for participation, horizontality and a new type of party that is more flexible, open, transparent and closer to the movements, parties are still different beasts operating on different political terrains. This does not necessarily mean that more horizontalist ways of governing will not be possible in the future, but for the time being horizontal practices seem at odds with governing as we know it. This would also resonate with left-populist theory: institutional politics and populist politics are based on two different logics.

Similarly, the populist aspiration of creating 'a people' does not seem to be enough in order to bring decisive changes to how parties operate. This was the case for both Syriza and Podemos. The Labour Party, on the other hand, though it did not manage to become the articulator of 'a people' outside its own structures (as we shall see later on, although it came close in 2017), it did create 'a people' within the Labour Party.[47] This was 'a people' limited to the ones willing to get a party card, but nevertheless a force that shifted the direction of the party. Although Momentum did inspire it to become a broader movement of social change, it remained tied by the confines of party politics which is not a huge surprise. As one member of the party leadership and supporter of Corbyn said:

> We are a serious party of government, we are the opposition of the government of the country for I don't know how many years – you cannot just have vehicles that are there to influence the direction of the Labour Party who are not party members. If we were just some far-left outfit that was nowhere near to come to power you can do what you want. But this is serious politics, this is the fifth largest economy in the world, if it is going to be the government of the country, this is going to be huge not just for Britain but for politics everywhere.

4

Left Populism at Elections: Rhetoric and Programmes

Populism has been seen as an electoral strategy, a method of communication and style of expressing demands used by politicians in order to win approval and votes and bring them to power. The policies they offer are trying to appeal to as many sectors of the population as possible, and they promise that their government will benefit 'us', rather than 'the elites', drawing an antagonistic division in society. In a way, this is how the electoral game has always been played: every politician promotes their vision of society – a programme that they argue will benefit the people. But for populism the creation of antagonistic frontiers is central. The aim is not to mislead the electorate or create a homogeneous society eliminating pluralism, but to bring about a pluralistic vision of democracy in which disagreement is taken seriously and the other is no longer an enemy but a legitimate adversary.

In this radical democratic vision power and antagonism are seen as part and parcel of politics and there is no promise of complete harmony.[1] For societies like those in Europe, bringing this about via the electoral route seems more plausible in the current historical moment compared to a revolution, although as I have said before the latter will also involve the creation of a people and antagonistic frontiers.

The process of actively creating 'a people' during elections is plausible when what I previously called a dislocation, a big rupture, has shaken the political bonds between the people and the political establishment. This, as we saw in previous chapters, is expressed at the grassroots level through collective action. This means that the previously dominant political, social and economic narrative is challenged – people are not buying it any more. In other words, the hegemonic vision of the world no longer sounds convincing.

For the political and economic system to function it needs our consent. Not in relation to this or that policy, but our more general approval that the direction of our society as a whole is the correct one (or, at least, the only possible one). Think, for example, of some of the 'truths' we all accepted that supported the neoliberal narrative before the crisis: 'investment' is good but 'expenditure' is risky, as much for countries as it is for individuals. The accumulation of debt is down to bad administration and frivolous individual behaviour. All these 'common sense' ideas are what allowed neoliberalism to be seen as the only game in town, and to some extent that continued even after the crisis revealed that the whole system was working less rationally than we had imagined and more on the basis of high-stakes gambling.[2]

Populism comes in at moments when this hegemonic vision is put into question and a new vision has to be articulated. For that to happen we need leadership and charismatic politicians who can sell this vision to the electorate.

Following on from Chapter 3 I now turn to the rhetorical and electoral strategies of Labour, Podemos and Syriza in order to examine how this vision was articulated on the terrain of parliamentary politics. Drawing on conference documents, party manifestos, interviews with party activists and my own notes and reflections recorded at the time, I explore how these parties with at least some populist elements in their narrative tried to create a new common sense and win their respective elections.

What becomes apparent is that the particular conditions have to be right to allow left-populist leaders to become plausible candidates. The most important condition in all the cases I am discussing here is the decline, or as in the case of Greece the total collapse, of the social democratic parties that were previously quite successful in winning elections in their respective countries. By the time of the crisis these parties had gone too far in embarrassing themselves by following the dominant neoliberal narrative.

Social Democratic Parties and the
Reconfiguration of the Political Terrain

What enabled the relative electoral successes of parties like Syriza, and to a lesser degree Podemos, was the decline of the well-established social democratic parties in Greece and Spain, PASOK and PSOE respectively. In the UK it was the decline of a particular direction that the party had taken with the ascendancy of Tony Blair that had brought it closer to the neoliberal consensus. It is true that the general idea of social democracy is based on a compromise between capitalism on the one hand and socialism on the other. This compromise had worn thin over the last 40 years as many social democratic parties across Europe started to pursue neoliberal policies. A key moment in this shift was the growth of the 'third way' in the Labour Party under Blair. One of the reasons for this shift is that after the offensive of Thatcherism and Reaganism in the 1980s even the left wing of the social democratic parties focused on defending what was left of the Keynesian welfare state rather than fighting for socialist policies.[3]

The reluctance or inability to fight for socialist policies has to be contextualised, and I discuss this in Chapter 5. Looking at the electoral strategies of the parties associated with left populism in Europe after the crisis, their relative gains are very much dependent on the decline of the previously dominant social democratic parties. The 2008 crisis found many of these parties in power – Labour in Britain, PASOK in Greece and PSOE in Spain – and they were inevitably blamed for a systemic crisis that went much deeper. That is not to say that they were themselves blameless. At that moment, when the need for social democratic policies alleviating the burden on the poor became a necessity, many of these parties embraced the policies of austerity, leading to significant electoral decline and in some cases total electoral annihilation. This process of embracing the neoliberal economic orthodoxy, however, had started decades earlier.

There is another reason why the fallen social democratic parties are important for our discussion: as in the case of PASOK, for example, they were the first left-oriented 'populist' parties of the post-dictatorship era. We should make a qualification here. The academic literature seems to conflate 'catch-all' centrist parties with populist ones that cut across diverse sectors of society. As I said earlier, all parties try to win a majority of votes. If, however, we look closer at the early days of PASOK, which came to power in 1981 and then alternated in power with the right-wing New Democracy, there was a moment when it was articulating a new vision, bringing the demands of the people to power, and it was positioned against a political establishment associated with Greece's authoritarian regime.

After the fall of the 1967–74 Greek military junta, PASOK became a new political force, one of the two parties dominating Greek politics – until the effects of the financial crisis and austerity measures kicked in. From its first landslide victory in 1981, PASOK was out of power only between 1989–93 and 2004–9.

In 2010 the then PASOK leader and Greek prime minister, George Papandreou, announced that Greece would sign a lending agreement (memorandum) with the Troika. PASOK's term in government had started triumphantly as they won almost 44 per cent of the vote in the general election of 2009. The 2012 election was a totally different story. PASOK came third with only 13 per cent of the vote, and ultimately formed a coalition government with New Democracy and the small centre-left party Democratic Left (DIMAR). The two elections of 2015 were then won by Syriza.

In the post-junta years PASOK had managed to present itself as the 'new left', differentiating itself from the communist left on the one hand and occupying the centre space left vacant by the disintegration of the old Centre Party on the other. Both communist parties in Greece (the KKE split in 1968 forming the orthodox KKE and the Eurocommunist KKE interior) had embraced the idea of a gradual transition to socialism, and PASOK's early commitment to 'third way' socialism fell somewhere between social democracy and Leninism.[4]

PASOK, which at that point had strong grassroots organisations, created a political frontier between the majority of 'the people' versus 'the privileged' oligarchy, the latter serving foreign interests and national elites.[5] Other things that contributed to the success of PASOK were its charismatic leader Andreas Papandreou (father of George Papandreou, who later led the party to oblivion) who used 'Change' as his electoral central slogan – not uncommon in electoral discourse, but often effective. For Greece in the early 1980s (PASOK was first victorious in the 1981 general election) the slogan signified the end of the ties with the dictatorship and the creation of a modern, democratic country. On the night that PASOK won, 18 October 1981, the main squares of Athens were flooded with people celebrating the true end of the junta and a new beginning. Even my family (moderate socialists but reserved in externalising their political opinions) joined those dancing until the morning and forgot my birthday, a scar I would carry forever despite my populist aspiration for a victorious 'people'.

In its early days PASOK advocated redistribution and social justice. Social justice in the Greek context aimed, among other things, at the incorporation into Greek society of those who had been excluded as communists since the end of the Second World War and the Greek Civil War that followed, and finally by the Greek junta of 1967–74. It was PASOK in 1982 that passed an amnesty law enabling the repatriation of those who had fled to the East European bloc during the civil war.[6] In this respect PASOK's populism somewhat resembles South American populism,[7] in that it brought those who had been marginalised back into the democratic process.

Also similar to South American populism, the question of national independence was central to the early PASOK – the founding declaration of the party on 3 September 1974 starts by condemning the expansionist politics of the Pentagon within the framework of NATO, and characterises the junta as backed by the US. A bit further down it argues that the root of this evil is the dependency of the country.[8] National independence is still a nodal point in the discourse of the Greek left. Dependency theory argues that the underdeveloped state of developing countries is due to their exploitation by developed ones. Organised around the centre–periphery division it still has a lot of resonance and forms the ideological reservoir of a section of the Greek left today.[9]

The 'dependency' argument often stands together with the inadequate development one, leading to the conclusion that progressive forces in government should further economic development and thus national independence, which when complete will make socialism possible. The outcome of this thinking is the weakening of anti-capitalist strategies, which has been the case for PASOK and the communist parties.[10] 'Inadequate development' was also part of the Syriza discourse when it came to power. Syriza, in line with the dominant perception of economics, did end up embracing the ideas of development and investment.

In the early days PASOK's programme was left leaning because it combined redistributive policies with the need for structural reforms. In terms of reforming the private sector the original strategy was the nationalisation of certain industries, a strategy that was abandoned by 1982. Instead it compromised with the creation of supervisory councils which would include representatives of all interested stake-holders such as management, workers, the state and local councils. By 1985 the turn to more orthodox neoliberal policies was fully underway and this was the period of privatisations, liberalisation and a commitment to a more efficient and flexible labour market rather than participation and redistribution.[11]

There are some striking similarities between PASOK in 1981 and Syriza in 2015, not only in how they became the acceptable, moderate face of the 'left' (or new left, if you want) but also in how they both weaved together the discourse of the 'enemy'. In both cases the enemies were multiple, domestic and foreign. For PASOK there was anti-imperialist sentiment in a country that had from its birth been economically and politically dependent on big powers propping up domestic right-wing elites – the 'economic oligarchy' – according to the founding declaration.[12] In the case of Syriza these powers were embodied in the institutions of the Troika that were invited to take control of the country by the now 'old' political elites, PASOK and New Democracy, via a memorandum.

It is true that many of the evils that would plunge Greece into the deepest of crises in 2010 had their roots in the policies of the later PASOK, a party that had moved away from its social democratic roots. The liberalisation of capital flows, for instance, was concluded in 1994 under a PASOK government. After the mid-1980s PASOK became less radical and more geared towards neoliberal economics, aiming at the supposed stabilisation of the economy. From 1995 onwards Greece saw an increase in GDP amounting to 61 per cent.[13]

Scandals of corruption, bribery and embezzlement, however, contributed to the party being progressively perceived as part of the corrupt oligarchy of Greece, even though a section of voters still recognised the achievements of PASOK, especially during the early period it was in power. On the one hand we had scandals associated with the private life of Andreas Papandreou himself, when he fell in love with a much younger woman, Dimitra Liani, who later became his wife. Although scandals around extramarital affairs are not necessarily related to the public sphere (though partners of politicians more often than not have quite a lot of political influence), they do contribute to the image of the leader, especially in countries where the traditional family is still relevant.

Besides these scandals, there were political scandals that stuck in the people's imagination, like the Koskotas scandal in the late 1980s. George Koskotas vaulted to power as the owner of the Bank of Crete and was a publishing baron among other things. He was accused of embezzlement and imprisoned in the US. PASOK had received a number of large donations from Koskotas and many party favourites had been employed in his publishing outlets. As a result the image of PASOK-related figures 'fleeing the country with suitcases full of money' is still part of the public imagination. The scandals continued, in the 1990s and the new century and there were allegations against both PASOK and New Democracy of receiving bribes from the multinational company Siemens in return for the firm being assigned projects funded by the Greek state. All these incidents, together with the shift from social democratic Keynesianism to austerity, contributed to the later collapse of the party which opened a space for Syriza.

PSOE, the social democratic party of Spain, had a similar trajectory, although it did manage to recover some of its power. The financial crisis of 2008 had profound effects in Spain and soon sparked a crisis of political representation that challenged the bipartisan system of the country. Both the socialist government of Zapatero (2004–11) and the conservative government of Rajoy (2011–18) had failed to respond to the crisis, and this is what, in 2014, enabled the emergence of Podemos and then Ciudadanos as forces in Spanish politics. Immediately after its creation Podemos won almost 8 per cent of the vote at the European Parliament elections and 21 per cent at the general election in 2015; Ciudadanos, a centre-right force (originally a Catalan party rejecting Catalan independence), moved further to the right as it entered the national political scene, winning 13.9 per cent of the vote at the same national election in 2015.

The process of decline had started for PSOE in the 2011 general election when the party suffered a huge defeat. Research has shown that if voting is determined by economics, voters more prone to take a centrist position are the ones who may more easily change party preference. Furthermore, the incumbent party's economic performance carries more weight in a voter's decision.[14] The same can be said in the case of PASOK, which was the incumbent party occupying a centrist position. The choices of the electorate are also dependent on how parties position themselves according to the left–right distinction, which I return to shortly.

What happened after the 2008 crisis, however, goes deeper. The dislocatory effect of the crisis led to voters to question the whole political establishment. That process was assisted by continuous corruption scandals, which from the crisis onwards were seen together with 'politicians, political parties and politics' as the most important problems in Spain.[15]

Apart from corruption there are other similarities between Greece and Spain. Both PSOE and PASOK came to power a few years after the respective dictatorships,[16] but in both cases parts of the elites from the dictatorships continued to run each country, occupying state structures and resisting democratic transformation. In Spain the victims of the Franco regime, for example, were not recognised and Franco's body was buried at the Valley of the Fallen mausoleum (together with many Republicans who fought him) until 2019. After that he was exhumed and moved to the less grand El Pardo-Mingorrubio cemetery. In Greece, apart from similar symbolic testimonies to the power of the dictatorship, there is also material assistance from Greek state institutions, like the army, for fascism/Nazism. It is alleged, for example, that the training of the death squads of the pro-Nazi party Golden Dawn took place in military bases, suggesting that the military is not free from powerful junta sympathisers.

Like PASOK, PSOE's social democratic credentials progressively shifted towards the neoliberal orthodoxy. Felipe González was instrumental in leaving behind the Marxist past of the party at the 1979 Extraordinary Congress XXVIII.[17] González went on to win successive elections between 1982 and 1996, with progressive achievements in healthcare and education, but also a departure from the original Keynesian programme in favour of neoliberal structural adjustment. Overall the record of PSOE in power is mixed. The adoption of third-way policies was partly the result of a lack of internal opposition as the party assumed the role of an electoral machine, as well as the absence of external opposition by the Communist Party of Spain, which resurfaced as part of IU in 1986.[18]

In 1984, although the party increased benefits for elderly and agricultural workers, it also lowered the maximum unemployment benefit and introduced temporary contracts.[19] Although in 1989 there was an expansion of the welfare state, in the 1990s the labour market was further deregulated. Still the party didn't feel threatened by the opposition.[20] That was until the defeat in the 2000 election. PSOE returned to power in 2004 with José Zapatero, who was responsible for advancements in civil rights but continued Gonzáles' economic policies, even going as far as having the same economic affairs minister, Pedro Solbes. In the 2000s, until the 2008 crisis, Spain enjoyed a comfortable economic environment which, as in other countries, created a real estate bubble that burst abruptly in 2008. As in Greece the conditions of the crisis created outrage against the two main political parties and opened up the political space to new political forces like Podemos.

Podemos activists always referred to these scandals, for example the 'black cards' of the executives of Caja Madrid, which supported their lavish lifestyles. In 2010 the bank merged with a raft of smaller banks to form Bankia, which was bailed out in 2012. Podemos activists used this example to explain what they meant by the term *la casta*, the network of political appointees in key positions with access to money and power – and which in some cases included figures associated with IU.[21]

Despite the early relative victories and the overconfidence of Podemos (which led them to reject alliances in 2015 in the belief that they could surpass the main parties), the opening for new political agents was about to get narrower for a number of reasons: the issue of Catalonia, where Iglesias accepted the premise of the referendum, the political shift towards more 'pragmatic' issues and other factors meant Podemos could not ultimately overtake the two main parties, PSOE and PP.

Leadership Contests and Leaders' Styles

There was, however, another factor that interrupted the electoral dynamic of Podemos, and this had to do with the PSOE leadership. This story has some similarities with the leadership of Jeremy Corbyn in the Labour Party. Parties are not unified entities; there are many internal struggles to define the direction of a party at any given moment. The term 'Pasokification', used too often to describe the demise of social democratic parties in Europe, is too much of a simplification.

After 2014 PSOE was losing power and it was itself afraid of 'Pasokification', as well as the possibility that it would be overtaken by Podemos. But Sánchez proved he could remain as the party leader after a turbulent period, and later formed a coalition government with Podemos in 2019. In October 2016 Sánchez had been ousted from his post following a bitter conflict within the party. His position, mandated by the federal committee, to vote against a new PP government brought him into conflict with the executive committee and half of its members offered their resignation. They believed that they had too few seats to form a government and were against the idea of forming one with Podemos. So Sánchez resigned – but then, in defiance of the party's old guard, he ran in and won the 2017 primary, showing that the rank and file of the party supported Sánchez's stance.

The most extraordinary story of internal party strife however in recent years has to do with the leadership of Jeremy Corbyn. The UK's Labour Party is a peculiar beast that contradicts the formal literature on parties that makes a crude distinction between 'vote-seeking' and 'policy-seeking' parties, the former focusing on maximising their vote, the latter interested in policies which are valued in themselves.[22] Labour is a party where the two come together: a particular way of thinking about politics that is sometimes called 'Labourism'. Labourism implies that the only vehicle for progressive politics is the Labour Party and, although trade unions have their place in the workplace, that it is the only representative of the working class. The only way for progressive politics and policies to be enacted is via winning elections and the job of the party is to deliver these majorities. In other words, nothing else (political movements, other parties, etc.) can bring about progressive politics and thus they are treated with suspicion.[23]

It follows that the fight for more left-wing policies will be an internal fight, and this is where Jeremy Corbyn comes in. The types of policies to be proposed and the prospects of delivering a majority are intricately connected. The effect of this attitude is twofold. On the one hand, it makes the possibility of coalitions very difficult. It is not that Labour won't form a coalition government, but rather that this will remain very instrumental and it is not something the party seems to contemplate before it is confronted with the possibility. On the other hand, any attempt to redefine politics or bring social change is internalised within the party. This is the significance of the leadership contest, especially with the 'one member, one vote' policy that made it more representative of the membership.

We can also argue that this is a two-way process. Organisational reforms were accompanied by changes in leadership that, since the 1980s, have signalled a shift to the centre. The most significant reform in recent memory was the removal of Clause Four in 1995, the clause in the constitution of the Labour Party that called for common ownership of the industry. This change under the leadership of Tony Blair opened the way for reconceptualising the direction of the party. Although Blair was very successful electorally – after all he was one of only half a dozen Labour prime ministers in the 120-year history of the Labour Party – he was not a left populist in the terms we are discussing in this book. He was popular and charismatic, no doubt, but his 'technocratic managerialism' has nothing to do with populism as a political logic, in fact it is exactly the opposite.[24] If Blairism was the next step towards 'modernisation' that had started with Neil Kinnock, a populist strategy would have been to mediate between Kinnock's politics and the radical Bennite alternative in order to bring electoral success. Blairism was not that. It was more the 'Pasokification' of the party, but at a moment when that could lead to electoral success.

Corbyn was very different in terms not only of his politics but also in his (ultimately unrealised) flirtation with populism. His attempt to create 'a people' aspired to bring to the electoral level the demands of all those who had been worse off after the crisis and the austerity policies of both Labour and the Conservatives, thus transforming the Labour Party into an agent of social change. This, however, never materialised.

The 2017 election played on this dynamic and Corbyn for some time was seen as the leader who would articulate this populist vision. Despite the predictions it was a relatively good moment for the Labour Party and Corbynism in particular. Although the party did not win, a surge in the polls increased its vote share to 40 per cent, which enabled the continuation of Corbyn's leadership. At the same time the Conservative Party lost its narrow majority, and while Theresa May remained prime minister it seemed that a Labour victory could become a reality next time. Things changed when Boris Johnson succeeded her as Conservative leader and a different type of right-wing discourse came into play, especially around Brexit.

A populist strategy was briefly pitched as a potential winning approach by Jon Trickett,[25] but the explicit engagement with populism was short-lived. Despite Labour's attempts to transgress different social divisions, the successful creation of 'a people' was related to the internal reconfiguration of the party, as discussed in Chapter 3, rather than the reality of the electoral terrain.

Podemos is the only party to draw explicitly on Laclau and Mouffe's theory of populism, although Mélenchon has also made references to their work, albeit appropriated in an ambiguous way.[26] The discourse of Podemos, at least in 2014–15, stressed the typically populist division of society into two antagonistic camps: 'the people' on one side and 'la casta' (the caste) on the other. By 2019 Podemos had agreed to form a coalition government with PSOE (previously considered part of *la casta*). In the early years, however, Podemos stayed clear of the establishment parties, and although clearly of a left-wing orientation it tried to bypass the left–right divide (which it sees as obsolete), appealing to all kinds of voters though the signifier 'the people'.

The divisions in Podemos' strategy have been structured around two leading figures of the party: Íñigo Errejón and Pablo Iglesias (the general secretary). The former, inspired by left-populist theory, would like to overcome the left–right divide and appeal to voters beyond that. This is why I believe Errejón was more open to a collaboration with PSOE as early as in 2015 in a bid to come to power and block PP. During the second 2019 election Errejón formed his own party together with Manuela Carmena.[27] Pablo Iglesias advocated the alliance with IU. IU rejected the proposal in 2014 but it did materialise two years later, in 2016, forming Unidas Podemos. The electoral strategy of Unidas Podemos was based on the assumption that the two parties together would achieve not the sum of their votes but a higher percentage that would allow them to surpass PSOE (known as 'el sorpasso'), but this did not happen. Instead it led to the loss of 1.1 million votes in the general election of June 2016 compared to the total of the two parties' previous votes in 2015.[28]

In attempting to reach sections of the population that had previously voted for establishment parties, one populist strategy was to rethink the left–right distinction. This was better articulated as an electoral strategy by Podemos, and was the preferred strategy of Íñigo Errejón. Podemos leader Pablo Iglesias was leaning more towards the left and this ultimately led to the alliance with IU. The 2019 alliance with PSOE was a further change of strategy, with Iglesias embracing Errejón's position but doing so with the left (IU) at heel. There are a number of reasons why in the case of Spain the left–right choice remained relevant: the left–right dichotomy is still the primary axis of party competition in Europe, and the main mechanism through which voters choose their party. Votes are still dependent on this identity.[29]

The Populist Political Frontiers

The main motto of the Labour Party's 2017 electoral campaign was 'For the Many, Not the Few', and for some commentators this was used as sufficient evidence of a populist strategy at play. Pitching 'a people' composed of diverse groups ('the many') against the elites ('the few') points to a conscious attempt towards creating an antagonistic populist frontier. Some have refuted that this indicated an attempt at a populist strategy, because 'the many' are not a 'unified singularity' but a pluralistic entity.[30] This is based, however, on the assumption that 'the people' is a unified mass, which as I have discussed is never the case. Rather 'the people' is the product of unifying different groups that never lose some of their separate identity (see the discussion in Chapter 1 on the creation of a chain of equivalence).

However, this attempt was not very successful in that the demands of different social sectors remained far apart. One possible reason is that Corbyn's leadership and campaigns exhibited an ambivalent relationship with class politics. On the one hand, Corbyn was evoking it (with references to Labour's 'northern heartlands'), while on the other it was trying to cut through class divisions in order to create a more inclusive 'us'. This ambivalence was more evident around the issue of Brexit, as we shall see in Chapter 6, but it also originates in the sharp intra-party divisions between Corbyn and his grassroots followers versus more centrist factions of the party (including the Blairites), and between Corbyn's close circle (dominated by ex-members of the Communist Party of Britain who are keen to keep a class-centred discourse) and other members of his shadow cabinet and supporters.

There was the assumption that electorally, one could either appeal explicitly to the working class and left behind (the victims of globalisation and turbo-capitalism) or appeal to Middle England and those citizens deemed to have 'aspiration' to get ahead and become socially mobile. The underlying assumption often seemed to be that appealing to one precluded the other, as if it was an either/or electoral strategy. Yet what has increasingly become apparent in recent years is the extent to which sections of the middle class in Britain are experiencing many of the problems with which much of the working class has long been familiar: increasingly precarious employment, stagnant pay, loss of autonomy and scope for creativity or job satisfaction in the workplace, due to increasingly authoritarian or macho-management, target-chasing and individualised 'performance' monitoring, while outside the workplace, previously affordable housing and free higher education are either increasingly priced out of reach, or necessitate incurring ever greater debt.[31]

How to communicate the increasing inequality on the 'us–them' axis was one of the key problems of Corbynism. With Boris Johnson succeeding Theresa May in 2019, and Brexit dominating political discussion, the dichotomy was articulated much more convincingly by the right, and especially Boris Johnson's right, which was very different from the previous hegemonic group within the party. Where the previous identity of the party was economically neoliberal and socially liberal, aspiring to a global order, the new faction was economically libertarian (or neoliberal on steroids), socially conservative and inspired by a new-found nationalism. Contrary to Labour, which felt obliged to have a very detailed programme offering policy alternatives on every conceivable issue, the Conservatives refused to answer any policy questions and instead repeated time and again the single key message: 'Get Brexit Done'. Policy decisions, including those related to Brexit, meant little to a public fed up with 'experts'. In reality, of course, Brexit was far from 'being done', not only because agreements with other partners (the EU included) were pending but also because the existing withdrawal agreement was far from sorted, as with the Northern Ireland border. However, Brexit as a signifier was vague enough that multiple grievances could see it as a solution. The clear vision, and the disregard for particular policies, gave the Conservative Party an unbeatable majority.

The 2014 Spanish European Parliament election was the first time Podemos enjoyed significant gains. What characterised their campaign was the simplification of the Podemos message, drawing on the distinction 'the people' vs *la casta* and strong emotional appeals as mobilisation mechanisms. Even the name of the party, Podemos (translated as 'We can'), and the mottos stemming out of that – for example, 'Yes, it is possible' ('Sí se puede') – had a strong emotional appeal to those who participated in 15M, bridging the party with the movements. Similarly their motto for the 2014 European elections – 'When was the last time you felt excited about voting?' – emphasised the bankruptcy of the politics of the establishment parties and created a strong mobilising appeal.[32]

This emotional appeal was coupled with the 'open-ended' or 'vague' nature of the signifiers used by Podemos, like 'democracy', 'justice', etc. This vagueness allowed different grievances to find a potential remedy in these signifiers. In other words, the discourse of Podemos was based more on the emotional appeal of 'vague' but appealing concepts and less on a detailed policy plan. The latter had two broad pillars: first, stop the politics of austerity, protect the welfare state and work for a more sustainable economy; second, get rid of corruption and open the way for constitutional reform.[33]

Two more things are important in terms of Podemos' electoral campaigns. First, the use of local networks of activists and local mayors endorsed by Podemos as central figures in the 2015 election. Spanish politics is determined by a multi-layered system which is very much shaped by the centre–periphery cleavage.[34] When 15M started to lose momentum we saw other grassroots initiatives emerge at local level such as Barcelona en Comú and Ahora Madrid with a strong anti-austerity agenda. Although Podemos didn't stand as such in the local elections it endorsed a number of mayors: Manuela Carmena in Madrid; Ada Colau in Barcelona; Pedro Santisteve in Zaragoza; José Maria González Santos in Cádiz. These very influential figures played a protagonistic role in the 2015 general election.[35]

Second, they ascribed much importance to communication strategies, a central aspect of every electoral campaign and yet one that is often not fully appreciated by anti-austerity, left-leaning parties.

The latter seem content to emphasise the hostility of the mainstream media which, although it can be a useful argument to cement one's anti-establishment character, does not necessarily engage with different publics. Podemos placed their communication strategy at the centre of their political project, bypassing the usual invisibility of anti-establishment small parties. This was achieved with a combination of their own audio-visual production and use of digital platforms but also with their presence in the mainstream media.

The importance of narratives was familiar to Podemos. They utilised a hybrid approach using traditional media like TV as a vehicle to create a 'common sense' narrative able to change the balance of political forces, and the digital platforms as a determinant of the organisational structures and a dissemination channel for their narrative, as I mentioned in Chapter 3.[36] *La Tuerka*[37] (the Screw) is the example cited in every paper analysing Podemos' success and a seminal case for effective dissemination of a counter-hegemonic message via alternative, digital channels and ultimately mainstream media. It was coupled with the controversial and confrontational message of Iglesias, which brought the mainstream media and Podemos into a symbiotic relationship.

In Greece the key moments of Tsipras articulating the diverse demands of the voters and creating 'a people' started in 2012, which ended with Syriza becoming first, the opposition, and then winning the general election of January 2015, the bailout referendum of July 2015 and the second general election in September 2015.

Before 2015, and as the possibility of being a serious contender for power came within its grasp, the party had undergone some serious transformations not only in terms of organisational structure (as I explained in previous chapters) but also in terms of its strategy and rhetoric. The decline of PASOK and the inability of New Democracy (which had formed a pro-bailout coalition together with the centre-left DIMAR) to offer solutions to the crisis, made possible on the one hand the formation of links between demands, identities and grievances and on the other the division of the political space into two antagonistic camps. The us–them distinction shaped the rhetoric of Syriza in 2012, with slogans like, 'They decided without us, we are moving without them' and 'It is either us, or them'.[38] This us–them distinction was aimed at the recovery of society according to 'the needs of the many rather than the interests of the few'.[39]

Similarly the construction of 'the people' at the January 2015 election was achieved by negating the differences between different sectors of the population. This negation appealed to the emotions experienced as a result of the crisis and the memoranda: 'Poverty does not discriminate, unemployment does not discriminate, despair does not discriminate'.[40]

The 2012 electoral strategy of Syriza (like Podemos) also evoked strong emotions and capitalised on the emotional energy of the indignant movement in Greece. This was achieved with references to the 'popular outrage' that brought about the election and the message of the movement to the establishment parties to 'go away'. At that point the enemy was both the national (PASOK and New Democracy) and the European elites which aimed at the 'limitation of popular sovereignty'.[41] The 2012 election was marked by the 'rage and the desire for the punishment of those responsible', but it was also vital to find a 'solution'.

As Syriza's 2012 proclamation argued (and contrary to the transversal strategy of Podemos), the solution would come from 'the left'. So Syriza, despite making an appeal to broad and diverse social groups, did not reject its left identity and in its programme was clear that it aimed to protect the most vulnerable while taxing great wealth and income. It proposed a four-part commitment: the recovery of the economy against 'the interests of the few' via social and environmental policies; the cancellation of the memoranda (via the mobilisation of the people); the enactment of policies that would benefit the most vulnerable – 'the unemployed, the low-income pensioners, the homeless' – and protect the public good; and the enhancement of democracy by giving voice to those who were up to that point voiceless.[42]

It is worth mentioning here that even in 2012 Syriza was not posing the question of 'Grexit'. The binary that Syriza tried to transverse, the game that it tried to change, was not moving away from a left–right distinction but rather to transverse the binary choice (expressed later both by EU officials and the left wing of the party) to either stay inside the eurozone with the memoranda or to leave the euro (even possibly leaving the EU). Instead Syriza argued that 'the dilemma of a memorandum or exit from euro and the EU is fake. They themselves [the

EU/eurozone] have confessed that their loss will be higher'.[43] This belief determined Syriza's strategy during the 2015 negotiations with the Troika.

It was also part of the way Syriza constructed its populist appeal during the 2015 election. As in his speech just before the January 2015 victory at the national elections, Tsipras' appeal to the Greek people was always connected with struggles of the peoples of Europe, such that, despite the memoranda and Troika, the Greek people were placed within rather than outside of the European historical framework: 'the history of our people, the history of all the peoples of Europe, shows us that a united people is never defeated'.[44] Tsipras reinforced the link between Greece and Europe by using mythological allusions:[45]

> Greece, our country, was, is and will remain the cradle of European civilisation. According to mythology, it was from this very place that Zeus abducted Europe. It is from this very place that the austerity technocrats want to abduct Europe again. NO. We tell them NO on Sunday. We will not leave Europe in the hands of those who want to abduct it from its democratic tradition ... From its founding principles – Democracy, solidarity and mutual respect.[46]

The references to Europe have a double objective: they place Greece within the European context but at the same time they register the need to reform EU institutions. 'There are those who've tried to portray Syriza as a threat to Europe. Don't listen to them. We will be the beginning for the major changes needed in Europe. Syriza stands for a better Europe.'[47]

So far I have shown how the political frontiers between 'us' and 'them' are articulated by parties of the left. There is, however, another dimension to this articulation which, for some commentators, is an exclusive political style that populist leaders exhibit.[48] Corbyn, even if not a populist, is an interesting example because he challenged the usual idea of 'charisma'. No doubt both Iglesias and Tsipras are great communicators. Corbyn less so, but he still managed to inspire a significant following early on in his leadership campaign. Corbyn was 'authentic', a powerful antidote to the charismatic style of Blair for example, which was now perceived as fake and dishonest. In a period when people were feeling they had been conned by politicians who were not really interested in their everyday concerns, Corbyn was perceived as a decent, principled individual. His style came as a sharp contrast to the emotionless and distant style of Theresa May and it was a key component of the attempt to create a link between the leader (Corbyn) and the people, by presenting the leader as one of them.

This image is true when it comes to many Labour members and most Momentum members, even possibly so for a young generation that was inspired by Corbyn's vision, leading to a 'cult sensibility' among his following.[49] The crowd erupting into chants of 'Oh Jeremy Corbyn!' at the 2017 Glastonbury festival testifies to how Corbyn, at least at that point, had captured the desire of the younger generation. Among those endorsing Corbyn were a number of cultural icons like the rapper Stormzy, who in Glastonbury 2019's historic performance (when he was the first solo black British performer to headline the festival) gave a very political speech against inequality, lambasting Corbyn's opponent Boris Johnson.[50] This appeal explains the results of the 2017 general election, but also the difficulty of moving from this particular audience to a wider audience that could swing the election in Labour's favour. The strong emotions Corbyn was evoking and his popularity among segments of the electorate were the reason behind the risky strategy to have Corbyn at the forefront of the election campaign in 2017.[51] It was considered risky because Corbyn's broad vision, at least in the early days (and possibly later on as well), was centred on direct action and protest rather than detailed policies.[52]

There were many attempts by the communications team of the leadership office to promote stories that would widen Corbyn's appeal as 'one of the people' for the wider electorate, which were met with differing degrees of success. Two of these stories were 'train-gate'[53] and 'jam-gate'. In August 2016 a video was released with Jeremy Corbyn sitting on the floor of a Virgin train, claiming it was 'ram-packed'. The video was used to support his policy of rail nationalisations, but controversy broke out when the company released CCTV pictures of the leader walking past available seats. He later explained that he was looking for two empty seats close to each other in order to sit with his wife. Despite the triviality of the story, or exactly because of that, it is emblematic of the new media environment and how a non-story comes to occupy the front pages and becomes an anchoring point for a particular policy debate. Although the story probably meant dif-

ferent things to those with pro- and anti-Corbyn views, it brought
to the forefront once again the state of the British railway network
and the failures of the privatisations of the 1990s. From a populist
perspective it demonstrated how the leader of the Labour Party is a
'common man' and it posed Virgin (and Richard Branson as the face of
the company) as 'them', the ones who are not part of us. In this respect
it could have contributed to the creation of an antagonistic frontier,
although it must have equally spread doubts about Corbyn's honesty,
at least among those who were either against his politics or against this
style of politics.

'Jam-gate' was a similarly controversial story in that it exposed on
the one hand that the mainstream media were not really warm towards
Corbyn, and on the other the weaknesses of his media team, especially
in managing crisis situations. Nevertheless, it was another successful hashtag on social media and another example of Corbyn's image
as one of the people, with all the flaws that this may hold. During
train-gate and after Virgin released its own explanation, Corbyn was
not available to comment for a period. Statements from Labour were
contradictory regarding his whereabouts, with one suggesting he
was unavailable because he was making jam.[54] Commentators in the
mainstream media used these stories to highlight Corbyn's supposed
incompetence, thus contributing to Corbyn's negative ratings among
voters.[55] Even the BBC contributed to the delegitimisation of Corbyn.
This process of delegitimisation occurred in several ways, according
to an LSE media report by Bart Cammaerts: (1) through lack of or
distortion of voice; (2) through ridicule, scorn and personal attacks;
and (3) through associations, mainly with terrorism.[56] This last alle-
gation of being associated with terrorism and thus being 'unpatriotic'
was something that many campaigners had to face during the 2019
election at the doorsteps. Apart from contributing to the reasons why
Corbyn didn't manage to get elected, it explains why many left-populist parties are at pains to find a place for national sentiments in
their discourse.

Lessons Regarding Election Campaigns

What can we learn from the electoral strategy of the parties associated
with left populism? The first lesson is that some had an opportunity

because of the historical conjuncture (like Syriza and Podemos) to find an opening in the political terrain as social democratic parties were not convincing anymore. This was more the case for PASOK than PSOE, and the difference may have to do with the stronger affiliation with the party that existed in the Spanish case but most importantly Sánchez's leadership and his perception of being mistreated by the old (corrupt) vanguard of the party.

This opening enabled the parties and their leaders to articulate an 'us–them' political frontier and to take votes from the constituencies of social democratic parties. This was not possible in the UK. First, in Britain the bonds with the political establishment were not severed in the same manner, and despite the anti-austerity sentiment there was not a deeper crisis of political representation. In other words, the financial crisis did not have the same dislocatory effect as in Southern Europe. Second, although in Britain there was the possibility of creating a political frontier between 'us' and 'them', this was easier during the first years of Corbyn's leadership when Theresa May was an uninspiring leader of the elite. This was not the case a few years later with Boris Johnson. Polls, although they should be treated with some scepticism, suggest that while in the 2017 election Corbyn's ratings were better than May's,[57] this was not the case in the 2019 election, when both he and Boris Johnson were very unpopular.[58] And yet between the two the public voted overwhelmingly for Johnson. His vision, like Trump's in a way, although dystopian for many, captured the imagination of different sectors of the wider public, while Jeremy Corbyn's remained confined to the Labour Party.

Finally, the media's coverage also played an important role, although the mainstream media have been hostile to all the parties I discuss here. The question is whether the communications office of the party has a strategy and how well the office can deal with 'crises'. One of the stories that kept on giving in the case of Corbyn was the antisemitism of the Labour Party. Things kicked off in 2018 when a row broke out regarding the adoption of the full International Holocaust Remembrance Alliance definition of antisemitism,[59] something that even Corbyn allies realised from the start would be like opening a can of worms. From a communications perspective, and although one would agree that the definition is problematic, the bad management of the story cost Labour a lot of bad press. Things got worse when allegations of antisemitism within the party were not dealt with swiftly. The charge of antisemitism against Corbyn may hold no truth but he still continued feeding the story even after a report from the Equality and Human Rights Commission in 2020, which concluded that there was harassment, discrimination and political interference in the Labour Party. Corbyn's supporters say he did so out of principle but communications experts know that with certain battles even if you win them, you lose. These stories have to be put to bed fast and a leadership team should prioritise its fights. Having said that, it is not always the case that this will work and there is no blueprint for dealing with hostile media; decisions should be taken according to the communication environment of each country.

5

The Institutionalisation
of the Populist Promise

In Chapter 1 I briefly discussed how populism is not an ideology with a particular programmatic content but a broad political logic that can be used by different populists: left, right, Greens, etc.[1] Who will articulate the popular will depends not only on the narratives employed but also on the correlation of forces: political, social and economic.

Our interest in left populism, however, demands that we examine its 'content' or, to put it differently, how the populist promise translates into a concrete policy agenda in the case of the left. Even if this agenda is clear in electoral manifestos do parties ultimately manage to implement it when in power? Are left-populist parties able to bring about radical change and in which areas? This discussion returns to some debates in Chapter 4 such as the role of the Keynesian economic policies of social democratic and left-populist parties in order to argue that the possibility of implementing a radical agenda lies in implementing policies that enable the reorganisation of production on the one hand and the ability of the grassroots to participate in politics on the other.

In most cases the European left moves between Keynesianism and a socialist alternative. Syriza, Podemos and Labour (under Corbyn), despite their particular histories and ideological reservoir, all shared an anti-neoliberal orientation (and in this respect a desire to protect and expand the welfare state) and an anti-capitalist/socialist vision.[2]

Let's turn to what happens to left-populist parties like Syriza and Podemos when they do eventually come to power. The question is not new by any means but it did resurface as some of these parties moved closer to electoral victory – and takes a central role when (or if) these parties come to power. In pragmatic terms what we have is the implementation of some Keynesian policies. Beyond that, on the issue of the democratisation of the economy (e.g. social ownership) there was not much progress. However, we have to take into account the particular impediments in each context.

More often than not merely coming to power opens up a world of criticism. The 'left' has for a long time moved between one strand – with a more revolutionary aspiration marked by hostility to the current system – and another (reformist) strand aspiring to a democratic transition to socialism. Needless to say that for the former the latter are 'traitors', while for the latter the former are 'delusional'. The reality, however, is that winning an election does not necessarily mean that one had made her/his ideas dominant in a given society and that state institutions will resist transformation. In this environment only a strong, grassroots movement will manage to support the government and demand a more radical change.

Drawing on Different Traditions

Before we look at the policies of Syriza, Podemos and Labour, let's start by examining briefly what 'socialism' (the preferred term in Britain) would entail and what the Labour Party is drawing from. The term socialism was purportedly first used in print in the *London Cooperative* magazine in November 1827, and progressively got more traction among the followers of Robert Owen. The term incorporated a number of previous demands, from the call for a new view of society to cooperative forms of economic activity, and stressed the essence of the new doctrine: operating collectively as opposed to individually in all facets of human activity.

Equality was central to socialism, political and economic. Owen's politics, for example, were shaped around the organisation of 'communities'. There the traditional notions of representation were suspended, and instead Owen insisted that participation in decision-making processes would be an unquestionable duty for all.[3] Permanent assemblies of all members of the community (rather than representatives or delegates) brought his ideas close to contemporary notions of direct democracy. It was 'the people' as the aggregation of all members of a community that would be responsible for self-governing.

Owen (and the English case in general) is a good example because from the early socialists to Marx the idea of how the new system would come about was divided between the question of 'reform or revolution'.

Despite the division across these lines of a number of socialist and left parties, both have something in common: a very different vision of society and economic production. This is different from accepting the existing (capitalist) system and aiming to mitigate its effects rather than changing it. The parties discussed in this book, socialist or left, have already accepted that the transition to socialism will be peaceful.

All the parties discussed here, left, socialist or social democratic, irrespective of how they define their identity, have accepted that the current configuration of the economy will not change drastically any time soon. Labour under Blair, PSOE and PASOK ditched their commitment to a socialist vision of society but they also failed to propose an alternative that did not broadly accept neoliberalism. We should not forget, however, that in terms of their origins both PSOE and Labour, despite belonging to the Party of European Socialists within the EU, are very different.[4] PSOE and other Southern European parties, be it socialist or communist, were in their inception Marxist. PSOE eventually denounced Marxism (see Chapter 4). Left parties like Syriza haven't, although it would not be widely contested to say that they are moving away from their Marxist origins (with the particular character it takes in different national contexts). When we think of Labour, however, the first thing that comes to mind is not Marxism but the trade union movement. One Labour Party officer and Corbyn supporter explains this difference:

Many of the other social democratic parties come from a Marxist tradition. The Labour Party doesn't. [...] The Labour Party was the creation of the trade unions because it was created in the first country to be industrialised, the trade union was the first mass movement [...] and the union leaders, all of them working-class men, understood they could win a strike but if they wanted to change society fundamentally in favour of the working people they should change the structures. They came together and created the Labour Party – and this is why still today, a hundred years later, 50 per cent of the conference vote is with the unions. [...] Afterwards of course, they talked to other thinkers like the Fabians or the Social Democratic Party of the UK, which was a Marxist party, and they all joined the Labour Party. So they brought socialism to the Labour Party.

The famous Clause 4 of the Labour Party was put together by the Webbs.[5]

The different origin of and the collaboration between social forces and groups within the Labour Party gives it its particular character and explains, to some extent, 'Labourism': the idea that only through the Labour Party is change possible. This is also what a famous quote attributed to Tony Benn suggests: 'The Labour party has never been a socialist party, although there have always been socialists in it – a bit like Christians in the Church of England.'[6]

The European socialist parties, however, were socialists at least in the way they were originally conceived. The Southern European parties in particular (like PSOE and PASOK), even after they denounced socialism, are shaped by the very specific Southern European context. Although they do not want to overthrow capitalism anymore they are not 'bourgeois' parties either because they are not accepted by the political establishment.[7] Others will disagree, arguing that this may have been the case for socialist parties before the Second World War, but by the time we get to the 1980s many of the socialist parties of the South are closer to social democratic compromise with the existing system.[8] In my view the first point is true if we consider the early years of these parties when they did have anti-establishment identities. In the process things changed.

We should not forget that many Southern European countries such as Spain, Portugal and Greece were subjected to authoritarian/dictatorial regimes and as a result the democratisation of the political system (and the inclusion of the socialist/left constituency in the community, which in many cases had suffered imprisonment, executions and exile) as well as the mitigation of social inequality took priority over their anti-capitalist rhetoric. The same can be said for the Eurocommunist parties that after the end of the radical demands of May 1968 conceded a strategic defeat.[9]

With that in mind, let's turn to the economic reform demands of Syriza, Podemos and Labour. What the socialist parties of the 1980s aimed at in economic terms is not radically different from Corbyn's manifesto proposals in 2017 nor from Syriza's, despite its particular Eurocommunist background, nor even Podemos (as Unidas Podemos) when they become a governing partner of PSOE in 2019. Most proposals move within the framework of Keynesian economics: increase government expenditure and support for health services and social services, increase the minimum wage, nationalisation and state subsidies for certain industries. These proposals come at a time, however, when the neoliberal consensus makes them sound more radical than they actually are – by no means did they signal a radical departure from the existing system. This is why certain parts of the Labour manifesto, for example, made references to the German or even US system: as a way to avoid the labelling of these measures as 'communist' or 'utopian'. We have to add, however, that Labour did move further, putting forward proposals for the democratisation of the economy. The 2017 manifesto, for example, takes issue with big banks and proposes a network of regional development banks: 'This new public institution will support a network of regional development banks that, unlike giant City of London firms, will be dedicated to supporting inclusive growth in their communities. The banks will deliver the finance that our small businesses, co-operatives and innovative projects need across the whole country.'[10]

The necessity to promote social control and different types of ownership (e.g. not only state ownership but community ownership too) was, according Eucleid Tsakalotos, Syriza's minister of economy from September 2015 to July 2019, recognised by PASOK in its early days in government and places the party at the left of social democracy: 'PASOK's approach [in the 1980s] can be termed left-wing social democratic in its awareness of the fact that, without institutional and structural reforms to promote various forms of social control of the economy, distributional initiatives (a better welfare state, higher wages, etc.) are always insecure.'[11]

The flagship policies of socialist and left parties after the crisis are nationalisations. The aim of nationalisations after the financial crisis was to remedy the catastrophic effects of austerity and clearly signal a departure from the neoliberal paradigm. The 2017 Labour manifesto, which was trying to articulate a populist division between 'the many' and 'the few' (as the title suggests), makes explicit reference to the return to public ownership of the rail, energy, water and postal services.

Despite the public perception of nationalisations as a 'left' issue, this is not always the case. In Greece nationalisations happened under Konstantinos Karamanlis' conservative government in the period between

1975 and 1980 (from banks to Olympic Airlines). In France the first two years of the François Mitterrand government, from 1981 to 1983, which some today will dismiss as not left enough, saw extensive nationalisations of financial institutions, banks and big industries.[12]

Going back to the Labour proposals what made the party's 2017 manifesto radical (and I think this has to be credited to John McDonnell's office) was, on the one hand and in accordance with Labour Party tradition, the incorporation of the cooperative sector into the future economic system, and on the other the attempt to go beyond nationalisation to a model for economic governance that includes employees and local bodies.

In terms of the cooperative sector the manifesto argues that the aim would be to double its size through the assistance of a new National Investment Bank: 'The National Investment Bank and regional development banks will be charged with helping support our cooperative sector. Labour will aim to double the size of the cooperative sector in the UK, putting it on a par with those in leading economies like Germany or the US'.[13]

The governance model is also interesting. The 2017 manifesto states that: 'In government, Labour would give more people a stake – and a say – in our economy by doubling the size of the cooperative sector and introducing a "right to own", making employees the buyer of first refusal when the company they work for is up for sale. We will act to "insource" our public and local council services as preferred providers.'[14]

The 2017 general election was when Labour came closest to power, and this was influenced by the dynamic created during the aftermath of the financial crisis by the widespread rejection of austerity. By 2019 things had changed, not only because austerity wasn't the right's main ideological frame, but also, as a Labour officer said to me: 'Austerity is not a big issue anymore [...] although public services are in a worse condition, people have seen their wages go up.' However, what is recognised as a big success for Corbyn (despite narrowly losing in 2017 and suffering a disastrous defeat in 2019) is that 'everyone in the Labour Party now accepts the case for a new economic settlement which is built around fair taxes, investment, as well as using the power of the state to generate economic growth and create fairness in society

[...] from the most right wing to the most left wing in the Labour Party, everyone accepts that and this is a huge victory'.

Although at the beginning of the anti-austerity movement the Labour Party was not a big inspiration for the European South because of the memory of Blair, the discussions around a different organisation of society were drawing (sometimes unknowingly) on the British cooperative history which is intertwined with the history of the Labour Party.

For early socialists, cooperatism and the establishment of retail trading societies were seen as a step towards the founding of self-governing cooperative communities, which for many of those involved in the movement was intended to be a form of emancipation from capitalism and the reign of middlemen.[15] Fast forward some 200 years and one of the most interesting experiments aimed at remedying the effects of the crisis in Greece was the creation of solidarity networks. Before the crisis, established institutions like the church and NGOs were offering some relative relief to those hit hardest by the crisis. Around 2011, however, activists (many of whom had been part of the indignant protests) started to run social pharmacies and clinics, food banks, direct markets and cooperatives.[16] This grassroots activity not only understood solidarity as an active, participatory way of engaging with politics but also as a way to experiment with new ways of organising economic activity. This was especially the case with the multiple eco-communities launched by young people who were looking for employment outside Athens and at the same time ways of deciding collectively within alternative economic structures.[17]

When these debates were sweeping across Greece I took part in many of the discussions held by Syriza organisations, occasionally pointing out (to the disappointment of some of the participants) that cooperative societies in Britain are not necessarily in conflict with the capitalist system, bringing the examples of Waitrose, John Lewis and the Co-operative Bank that evolved from such origins.

In Britain, however, despite the long history of cooperatism, the effects of the crisis were managed not by spontaneous grassroots activists (as many but not all in Greece) but by NGOs. Food banks, for example, are charitable services in Britain, without the broadly political considerations of the equivalent solidarity networks. Furthermore, in some instances they have been seen as a site open to entrepreneurial exploitation, as is the case of the Foodbank app launched in 2014 by Miriam Cates, now a Conservative MP, which charged food banks a fee to join.[18] This again points to the differences in the terms of both grassroots activity but also of the effect of the crisis in Britain and Greece. The first is that the crisis had dramatic effects only on particular sectors of British society, sectors that had been continually assaulted by neoliberal economics, but it did not have the same severe effects on others, as was indeed the case in Greece and Spain. The second difference is that the solidarity networks in Greece or the actions against home repossessions in Spain were part of the wider movement. As I mentioned before, comparing the anti-austerity movement in Greece/ Spain and the United Kingdom is misleading because in the latter case there was some grassroots activity but not a wide movement as such.

Fighting against Austerity: From Grassroots to Policy

Scholars argue that an important factor in trying to democratise deregulated markets is social capital, including trust or norms like reciprocity. These enables the creation of a long-term strategy that will socially regulate the market and help to deal with issues of opportunistic behaviour that thrive when economic regulation is weak.[19]

In Southern Europe, however, deregulated markets are intertwined with 'kingship' relations that have become a big part of establishing the dominant class and are used by politicians in order to secure electoral victories. Southern European institutions and the public sector are dominated by employees who were rewarded for voting for one party or another. It is no secret that since the nineteenth century clientelist relationships between politicians/parties and the electorate have been a dominant feature in Greece.[20] On the one hand, this is a problem for the institutionalisation of a new economic framework. Even if a party like Syriza attempts to create new legislation it is questionable whether this legislation will bring together the government and social organisations in a mutual partnership that will promote a new economic framework. On the other hand, countries like Greece lack autonomous trade unions, consumer organisations and local authorities that could work towards this aim. Even between these groups, let alone between them and the government, there is mutual suspicion.

What we are left with is vertical, hierarchical structures that foreclose the adoption of new long-term strategies.[21]

This debate opens up some interesting areas for discussion in relation to left populism. The first is how possible it is to implement policy in countries with the characteristics I mentioned earlier regarding Southern Europe. The second has to do with finding a solution to left populism's 'verticality': rather than having decisions and change imposed from the top, it would enable more horizontal, bottom-up processes and in this way democratise politics and the economy. An answer to these questions can be traced back to the solidarity networks that emerged during the crisis.

Solidarity became the primary trope under which many indignants started to organise on a grassroots, local level beyond the square protests. In every neighbourhood solidarity groups started to spring up. Almost all solidarity group members had been part of the 'Aganaktismenoi' (Greek *Indignados*) protests and in many cases they were the initiators of these efforts. Pre-existing alternative social and cultural centres, and political and neighbourhood networks, took a new direction and engaged in solidarity initiatives. The two events – the protests and the creation of more permanent solidarity networks that tried to mitigate the effects of austerity like food banks and social clinics – are something that the activists themselves treat as the expression of the same desire to help, but also to change the way things were operating up to that point. Activists explain, for example, how some doctors who helped at the Syntagma Square first-aid station were founding members of the social clinics. Others describe their state after the protests as 'restless'. One interviewee recalls how he and other members of a social centre who had no previous experience in food distribution decided to bypass the commercial circuits of the supermarkets and travel to the north of Greece, in order to meet producers and set up food distribution without mediators. This points to how these initiatives became experiments for a different type of economic organisation with a cooperative orientation. In the process the political identities of the activists themselves were transformed, connecting solidarity with 'socialist', 'leftish', 'democratic' principles and ethics.

Even in initiatives like eco-communities and cooperative shops, despite their bottom-up organisation, the issues of verticality persists. This was one of the reasons behind the creation of 'Solidarity4All'.[22]

The aim of the organisation was to create a site mapping that represents all solidarity groups online, increasing their visibility and reach. The initiative respected the autonomy of each individual initiative and it remained leaderless (despite the appointment of paid organisers, which does suggest that these organisers had some privileged position and voice).

For the participants in these initiatives the organising logic behind Solidarity4All was horizontalist. As one of the organisers explains, 'It has the same logic as that behind both social media and movements. A logic which goes against the logic of the state, the logic of the political parties or the older organised movement which operated on a different logic.'

For both Syriza and the European left, social and solidarity economies is (at least in rhetoric) central to their vision of a type of growth based on equal relations of production. In policy terms, however, despite some good bills from the Syriza government, these types of experiments remain embryonic.[23] And yet they would be a more radical vision through which the left could differentiate itself from social democracy (although many social democrats are also in favour of such a direction).

Euclid Tsakalotos, minister of finance in the Syriza government and member of one of the Syriza tendencies mildly critical of the leadership team, has urged the European left to discuss alternative models of production based on cooperative principles and the examples of solidarity economies and energy communities. According to him the Syriza government supported these types of experiments, but he also stated that there are two important questions in relation to these issues. First, are these models only part of the solution or a holistic solution? Second, are there the necessary human resources at local level to showcase the importance of these experiments for the local economy?[24] The right-wing Kyriakos Mitsotakis government that succeeded Syriza was openly hostile to these experiments, serving an eviction notice to one of the biggest social surgeries, Iatreio Ellinikou, in February 2020 without attempting to rehouse what was one of the exceptional solidarity efforts during the crisis of 2008.[25]

Let us then turn to the implementation of policies by left-populist parties at the national level. Despite the defeat and the signing of the memorandum in 2015, the Syriza government committed itself in

September (after the second election) to implementing a 'parallel programme', a programme that would run alongside what had been agreed in the memorandum and would have a twofold aim: first, to mitigate the consequences of the memorandum for the waged, self-employed, unemployed and retired; second, to strengthen the position of those strata, politically through democratic reforms, and economically by opening the way for disengagement from neoliberalism and austerity policies. The three main axes that would make this possible were the reform of the institutions and the democratisation of the political system, the re-establishment of the welfare state with an emphasis on the protection of the more vulnerable strata, and the creation of foreign policy that would be based on the pursuit of peace.[26]

In brief, the programme had four pillars: the first had to do with mending the effects of the humanitarian crisis, the second with the restarting of the economy and tax justice, the third with the creation of new jobs and the fourth with the transformation of political institutions.[27] When in government some of Syriza's immediate policies minimised the catastrophic effects of the crisis, especially for the most vulnerable, but unemployment remained high (even if slightly decreased) and state institutions remained as corrupt, undemocratic and unfit as before.

It is true that Syriza could not implement many of its policies after a painful negotiation (which Syriza entered totally unprepared or, as some argue, with naïve expectations) leading to the signing of another memorandum in summer 2015. Furthermore, it proved that the institutions, colonised by a political class hostile to any reform, and especially any reform coming from a 'left' government, would resist and persevere. Finally, it was Syriza's own adaptability to institutional reality (and especially the reality of becoming a governing party) that put an end to a more radical potential.

More specifically, the government of Samaras–Venizelos (New Democracy and what was left of the old PASOK) had agreed back in 2012 to mid-term measures lasting until 2018. These measures demanded huge surpluses from the Greek economy and by 2014, knowing that Syriza was approaching power, they stopped implementing any of these in order to bring Syriza to an impasse when dealing with an economy that had been totally destroyed and an empty treasury. Their aim was to create a situation where a left government would only last for a short interim period.[28]

Within this framework, what the Syriza government lists as its achievements in the first two years in power are: the avoidance of the total collapse of the pension system, the granting of the thirteenth wage of Christmas 2016[29] the avoidance of cuts in health and education that had been scheduled in 2014, not carrying through the doubling of the price of electricity and water which the Samaras–Venizelos governments were committed to and stopping further sales of public property.[30]

The reality was less rosy, although most will recognise that Syriza did try to protect the most vulnerable from the crisis as it had promised in its manifesto (the first pillar) before the signing of the memorandum. Looking at the privatisations of Greek infrastructure for example, Syriza did implement them (some argue with better terms, others disagree), a process that was accelerated when Syriza lost the general election of 2019.

When in 2019 the right-wing government led by Mitsotakis won the general election, one of their main pledges was that they would move forward with privatisations, a promise that later on proved less ambitious due to the lack of interest in the energy sector, property development of state assets and the remaining state-owned ports, the most desirable sectors.[31] Privatisations, the neoliberal flagship promising that privatised companies offer cheaper and more efficient products and services, has been proven a lie time and time again – but during the crisis the debtors insisted on the selling of public assets. This is not to say that the public sector in Greece is not highly problematic. It is not only inefficient but also a bargaining chip between parties and their clientele, either in the form of rewarding voters with positions in the public sector or other private interests via lucrative contracts. What I want to suggest, however, is that in the case of Greece, as in most other cases, the imposition of privatisations led to the loss of assets but not real growth. Some of the privatisations that the Syriza government was forced to implement were the selling of the Piraeus port to the China Ocean Shipping Company (COSCO), which was the only bidder; and the leasing of 14 local airports to the German company Fraport. The gain from these privatisations for the Greek state is questionable. It has been argued, for example, that the price of

368.5 million euros paid by COSCO is very little and by the end of the lease the Greek state will have lost 700 million euros. The reason is down to two of the three container companies operating in the port since 2008, which are COSCO subsidiaries. Since 67 per cent of the port's shares were sold to COSCO, it is COSCO that will receive fees from them rather than the Greek state:

> This calculation is double-dealing, as until now the OLP (operating company of Piraeus port) has received an annual lease cost of around 35 million euros from the COSCO subsidiary for the two container terminals. 67 per cent of this money will now go to the majority shareholder of OLP, i.e. from one of COSCO's pockets into another. This means the Greek state will lose out on at least 700 million euros by the end of the lease, which should have been deducted from the 'total value' of OLP's privatisation.[32]

In Spain the beginning of the Sánchez (PSOE)/Iglesias (Unidas Podemos) government aimed to reduce inequality by introducing a minimum basic income, guaranteeing an income of 462 euros with additional benefits for families up to a maximum of 1,015 euros per month. Iglesias spoke about the new measure as a historic decision for democracy, where 'a new social structure is created'.[33] The scheme could affect up to 2.3 million people and it is a significant move in a country hit hard by the 2008 crisis and expecting a GDP contraction of around 9 per cent in 2020 due to the coronavirus crisis. The 1978 Spanish constitution bestowed on regions the power to implement social assistance, and many regions had failed to assist those meeting the necessary criteria. Although some economists welcomed the move as an experiment in universal basic income, in reality the policy is aimed at the poorest, not universally.

Apart from these economic policies, however, the reform and democratisation of the institutions of democracy remains a big problem for left-leaning governments.

The Syriza government had to battle not only the implementation of these programmes but also and most importantly the vested interests behind many of the policy decisions that allowed little space for more systemic transformation. To give you an example from the health sector, which has resonance with many other countries including the UK, when Syriza came to power it abolished the 5 euro ticket price for using public hospitals.[34] Equally important was the inclusion within social security of those in part-time employment, the chronically unemployed and elderly people who were not covered by national insurance.[35] What we see here is that to an extent it was possible within the memorandum framework to protect the most vulnerable parts of society, and that Syriza did try to mitigate some of the cynical measures that the Troika and the previous governments were eager to implement. However, the issue that attracted most attention during the time of the Syriza government was the Novartis scandal, which involved the bribery of Greek politicians by big pharmaceutical companies.

Novartis, a Swiss pharmaceutical company, was accused of bribing Greek politicians in return for patronage. In February 2018 the Greek Parliament decided to investigate this alleged case of corruption and those associated with it – such as Yannis Stournaras (governor of the Bank of Greece at the time), Dimitris Avramopoulos (Europe's migration commissioner) and the previous prime minister, Antonis Samaras – who were suspected of giving Novartis preferential treatment. The investigation was handed to a cross-party committee before they could be prosecuted. Those accused called it a 'big conspiracy' against Syriza's opponents. Although Novartis admitted bribing doctors to prescribe more pharmaceuticals in a number of countries and agreed to pay $347 million for violating the US Foreign Corrupt Practices Act in 2020, the allegations of Greek bribes were not included in the case.[36] In an interesting twist, in July 2020 (while Syriza was in opposition) the Greek corruption prosecutor Eleni Touloupaki responsible for the Novartis case was put under criminal investigation, ordered by the head of the prosecutor's office.[37] The independent 'estates' of liberal democracy (judicial, executive and legislative) are very closely intertwined in Greece and other Southern European countries, as the next case also suggests.

Other scandals indicating that resistance from vested interests is not solved by simply electing a left government and passing a few bills – at least not a government that is disassociated from a well-organised and active grassroots that can rally the support of society as a whole – are related to the Greek media landscape. The development of Greek (and other Southern European) media has a particular trajectory that differentiates it from the Western liberal media. Some have called this system the Mediterranean or polarised pluralist model, with weak professionalisation, state interventions and close bonds between politicians and journalists.[38] The power of Greek media moguls and their influence on Greek politics is unprecedented in other European countries. Even the public sector broadcaster (ERT) is more each government's ally than a (relatively) objective outlet.

One of the first measures of the Syriza/ANEL government in 2015 was the reopening of ERT, which had been closed down in 2013, a decision that sparked a wave of protests at the time. The resistance of ERT employees had been seen as a struggle against austerity itself and it attracted widespread support within (and outside) the country. Private media were also in danger of closing down. One newspaper of the few representing the centre-left, *Eleftherotypia*, closed down and a number of others fell into financial difficulty.[39] The TV channel MEGA stopped transmitting progressively between 2016 to 2018 and hundreds of employees were made redundant without receiving their wages or any redundancy payments. When the channel opened again in 2019, under the right-wing government of Mitsotakis, the new owner Marinakis did not pay the debts of the previous owners towards those who had lost their jobs or offer any form of re-employment.

But for left journalists, the decisions of the Syriza government were not flawless either. One of them said to me:

Syriza had a wrong policy in relation to the media in three issues. The first issue has to do with its own media like Kokkino radio, Avgi. It should immediately realise that all other media would be against them and that they had to protect and support their own media in order [to have a vehicle] to explain the Syriza government's policies. The second is that Syriza should immediately say that ERT will become like [the] BBC. Not supporting the party, but in terms of principles. [...] And the third is that they [Syriza officers] believed we should have good or bad relationships with editors. We shouldn't have neither good nor bad. We should have formal.

What is desired here is not far from some widely accepted principles of liberal democratic media, even if those are failing us in most countries. To allow the Syriza government to 'put in order' the Greek broadcasting framework, one decision made was to reduce the number of national TV channel licences to four, later revised upwards (after pressure) to seven. The number of channels was decided according to the size of the advertising market in Greece and it was meant to ensure that all of the main channels (excluding local and specialist ones) were economically viable. Furthermore, in order to move away from the system of 'temporary licences' that previously allowed TV station owners to avoid the licence levy, the Syriza government invited owners to register their interest and bid for the licenses. The starting price for a licence was 35 million euros. The fight between the government and the political establishment/owners that followed could be the plot of a Hollywood legal drama. The first auction in 2016 was cancelled because it was found that it should be the Broadcasting Council rather than the government which gives the broadcasting licences. The problem was that the right-wing New Democracy opposition was refusing to consent to the appointment of the council (this body has to be formed by agreement with the opposition party).

The fierce war between the telecommunications ministry[40] and the private TV owners continued through the second auction in 2018 – this time the licenses were granted by the Broadcasting Council. In the end the Council of State confirmed the legality and constitutionality of the second licensing process.[41] That did not stop the Greek media moguls, who now tried to delay paying the yearly licence instalment, from hoping that the government would change (as it did in 2019) and everything would go back to business as usual.[42]

The case of Syriza is important for understanding the shift from grassroots activity to policy making. Although the grassroots became important laboratories of alternative economic policies during the crisis, when in power Syriza (admittedly in very difficult circumstances, constrained by the memorandum) tried to implement policies that would protect the most vulnerable and would correct some of the problematic Greek institutions. The resistance from the establishment was fierce and the position adopted was more defensive rather than one of leadership. A saying that was used a lot by Syriza (sometimes as a genuine reflection, sometimes as an excuse) is that 'being in government does not necessarily means that one has the power'.

How Do We Want to Be Governed?

In his lectures on biopolitics, Foucault proposed an interesting critique of the left, arguing that it hasn't really advanced a new logic of governing.[43] His lectures examined the shift from classical liberalism (Adam Smith) in the nineteenth century to the early thought of neoliberalism in the twentieth century. The latter put in motion a new logic that ties together the market and the state, a logic not restricted to economics but to a whole new logic of governing too. There he also advances a brief critique of the left, namely that it lacks such a logic. Some may find this position unfounded and they will no doubt reference a list of left proposals of governing, such as workers' councils and so on. I tend to agree and disagree with them. On the one hand, as I explain shortly, I believe that the radicalisation of a left project is exactly this more local way of governing, like municipalism. At the same time, all the cases I examine in this book seem to find it difficult to avoid the pitfalls of the usual centralised logic of governing when in government.

Both Syriza and Podemos officials talk about how these two parties changed to something less radical when they came to power. In terms of Syriza, one interviewee described how the party got 'governalised', meaning that when in power it accepted the same hierarchical structures and practices, while its grassroots became resigned to inactivity:

> The party got governalised [...] What Syriza didn't do is to work within society in order to re-enforce its connection with the grassroots. The latter would in return demand [more radical change] from the Syriza government. This is what the local organisations didn't do. If they had done that, in my opinion, we would have a different clout at the elections [2019].

A similar shift is also identified in Podemos. As an ex-officer of Podemos explains:

> I can't understand what Podemos is doing at the moment [2019]. I really can't. At the same time I am not sure if outside Barcelona, Ada Colau and the people around her, which I think they are working really well, even in that case I am not sure if what we used to call

the 'space of change', I don't know if that political space is actually working anymore. I feel distant. I do respect them and I do want them to do well, to be successful as much as they can but I don't understand what anyone is doing.

Let me now try to summarise the argument of this chapter. For different reasons the left parties under examination seem to operate within a social democratic framework, and despite some more radical proposals (as in the case of Corbyn's Labour, though it did not come to power) they are more or less trying to mitigate the extreme inequalities of the existing system. Their moment was after the crisis of 2008, and the imposition of austerity and neoliberal adjustments that worsened an already desperate situation. What could have been done differently, especially when it comes to Syriza but also for Podemos and Labour, was to reconnect with the grassroots and enable a more 'horizontalist' way of engaging in politics and of organising economic activity.

This debate has been central for left populism and for radical politics, and it is part and parcel of our assessment of these parties. Many argue that left-populist parties are too vertical, decisions are taken top down and the governing logic they demonstrate when in power is the same as any of their predecessors. Being more horizontal means allowing the grassroots to participate in governing, but at the same time promoting economic and other policies that allow for such a change. The demand for the formalisation of popular dissatisfaction into policy was present in the Indignados movement in Spain, but the fact that electoral support for Podemos, as discussed earlier, came with the centralised management of the party is not very promising.[44]

Spain, like Greece, developed practices that went beyond simple demonstrations, for example the so-called *escraches*: a movement to protest the evictions of people who could not pay the mortgages on their homes. This movement organised itself in the same way as the initial Indignados protests: horizontally, through social networks and so on, and it referred to itself as a 'platform' (*Plataforma de Afectados por la Hipoteca* – mortgage victims' platform). The protesters would show up outside the homes of people threatened by eviction, thereby trying to prevent the authorities from kicking people out of their homes. Stopping evictions became part of Podemos' pledges but also the Syriza government's policy. The former achieved the halting of evictions at the municipal level through the 2015 election of Manuela Carmena in Madrid, who overturned the evictions of many families living in social housing and safeguarded rental contracts.[45] Syriza, on the other hand, as a governing party, opted for the top-down approach through a legal framework that would protect the first or main residency of those in dire economic conditions from auctioning (after a court application and a debt settlement).[46] The auctions were part of the memorandum agreement with the EU and IMF, and soon protests against the auctions led by the left groups who walked out of Syriza in 2015 became a common feature of grassroots politics. Syriza was of course between a rock and hard place, but at the same time it had lost support among grassroots activists. There are significant differences between Podemos (which was not in national government and had a strong presence at municipal level) and Syriza (which was trying to implement a parallel programme while confined by the demands of a memorandum). In terms of national governance though, both parties adopted a top-down approach when in office. The promise of participatory, horizontalist politics was only present at the municipal level, where some relative gains in that direction become reasons for hope.

Gains at Municipal Level

What is municipalism? Some describe it as a new social movement aiming to transform the local state and economy and to promote democratic autonomy, from town parishes to big cities.[47] Where national politics seems even after the crisis to follow a predictable trajectory that does not challenge the neoliberal paradigm in any radical way, the argument runs, most contemporary victories happen at municipal level. The US sanctuary cities movement has forced municipal governments to shelter immigrants and refugees, while in Turkey the communist mayor of Tunceli (apart from restoring the Kurdish name of the town) set out to create a cooperative food system.[48]

Historically, municipalism has a long history which often reads as a precautionary lesson. Many municipalist projects were progressively formalised into less radical endeavours. Transnational municipalism was progressively absorbed into EU network initiatives such as Eurocities. Although these institutional turns of municipalism are differentiated from more radical experiments and designated as 'pragmatic' or 'entrepreneurial',[49] there is a point to be made about how initiatives with a radical edge are progressively absorbed within less radical institutional frameworks. Cooperatism is another example, which is very much intertwined within the logic of contemporary municipalism.

Contemporary interest, however, focuses on projects which for the time being have a more anarcho-socialist and ecological orientation, challenging neoliberalism, capitalism and a state-oriented logic. Such an approach is indebted to the work of Murray Bookchin[50] but there is a long list of authors like David Harvey who view contemporary municipal experiments as having revolutionary potential.[51]

Barcelona en Comú is one of these contemporary examples, connected with the politics of Podemos: activists and theorists, aligning themselves with a left project to be governed by the people, radicalised politics from the bottom up, creating this municipal platform that elected Ada Colau mayor of Barcelona in 2015.

The turn to municipalism rather than electoral politics at national level is underpinned by 'a radical-reformist orientation towards the local state' and it is perceived as a challenge to state logics and state politics.[52] The city carries a new promise, and Harvey argues that the 'the right to the city' is the right to change the city, to create structures that enable participation and inclusivity and oppose the logic of neoliberalism.[53] Correctly in my view, municipalism challenges the adequacy of the nation state to continue to play the dominant position it has enjoyed for the past couple of hundred years, and it is not coincidental that aggressive neoliberalism and economic globalisation have led to a proliferation of demands for independence, from Scotland to Catalonia. In terms of left populism, municipalism can be a more interesting site for the articulation of the people and it can be a more fruitful way of dealing with the dichotomy between top-down (vertical) and bottom-up (horizontal) approaches that divides theorists like Laclau from those like Michael Hardt and Antonio Negri.

Equally, despite the desire to use municipalism as a way to go beyond the nation state, there is no reason why a left national electoral strategy would not consciously use the potentiality (electorally and organisationally) of the city as a way of devolving power and enhancing the democratic participation of the people. This is what happened in Spain when activists from the 15M movement, neighbourhood associations, academics and others came together to shift the challenge of the movements to a different level by taking over municipal institutions in order to put them 'at the service of the majority and the common good'.[54] The identifier 'En Comú' marks the distinction between 'the commons' (resources that are the common property) and the capitalist and nation state logic of the 'enclosure' (taking over what was held in common for the exclusive use of private owners), showing how one stands in clear opposition to the other. Note how the majority/minority dichotomy is transported from national to local politics. The most well-known example is Barcelona but it is by no means the only municipal success; Ahora Madrid is another, even if very different, example of municipal control.

These platforms, aiming to win at local level, had certain characteristics like: '(i) plurality of actors, (ii) pragmatic solidarity based on a small number of shared values (a minimum), and (iii) promoting and using a new way of doing politics'.[55] Again it is interesting to see how some of these characteristics seem to map the process of creating a chain of interests – a chain of equivalences as I called it in Chapter 1 – which is part and parcel of the emergence of a populist subject. Anarchists, leftists and Greens come together, they become 'a people' that stands against the vested interests of the city. They connect based on some shared values even if their particular identity is not totally neutralised and homogenised. Although the theorists describing these processes are interested in social movements rather than populism, the process could be used as an illustration of Laclau's theory. They argue that 'historical differences and ideological disputes were deliberately left to one side, and instead efforts concentrated on finding shared activities and policies which were agreeable to all the main groupings, even if they supported them for different reasons. By sharing in participatory and prefigurative practices, shared values develop.'[56] The face of this initiative and the embodiment of this process is Ada Colau, a named leader.

There could be an objection here. Are we discussing a populist logic or a mere progressive alliance? This would depend on the type of identification with the project. If it transverses the previous identities of the original groups to become one (albeit not a homogeneous mass), coming together and leaving behind their previous identities and forming a new one in the process, then it is not a mere alliance but could be a populist project, depending of course on if and how a new political frontier is being formed.

The politics of this new formation borrows from the experience of the indignant movements, from anarchist theory and from ideas of direct democracy. Municipalism becomes a bridge between the movements and local electoral politics, even if electoral victory is not an end in itself but rather a way of testing socialist policies.[57] Moving to the level of municipal politics entails many dangers, of course, which are controlled by a number of mechanisms such as limiting the salaries of those in office and using social media in the electoral campaigns – mechanisms which were also incorporated (or promised to be) in the national politics of both Podemos and Syriza, although to different extents. As with the other discussions in this book the problems of electoralism and verticality remain, but these municipalist experiments are the only way to actively engage and promote a new, participatory type of politics that will bring change at the local level. Apart from governance by its own members (rather than national political centres or international NGOs) and the rejection of top-down politics in these municipal initiatives, it is the new ethos of contemporary municipal experiments that is against competitiveness and patriarchal relations.[58]

In May 2018 Ada Colau addressed the Fórum Europa de Nueva Economía about how the city is working to maximise its potential by attracting talent and productive investment, but not neoliberal speculative investment.[59] Some examples of productive investment setting up in Barcelona included a Facebook centre to combat fake news and the first Moodle headquarters in Europe.[60] The city also stands in an adversarial relationship with the state and national policies, with its refugee programmes for example:

> Cities and towns are where refugees are received and integrated, but in Spain they have no say in asylum policies and do not receive any funding to implement them. The state does not finance any local integration policies, although it does receive EU funds for this purpose. The amount set aside for 2014–2020 is over 330 million euros.[61]

The city site also includes practical information on how to help with refugees, citizens' message boards and more. Although one cannot guarantee the trajectory of these municipal laboratories, they seem to involve some interesting experiments on social and economic policy.

To sum up, there seem to be a number of areas of contestation on the rare occasions that left populist parties come to power. The first is that they seem to emerge when social democratic parties are declining, often due to their adoption of neoliberal policies. When this happens the left parties seem to move to 'occupy their space', remaining within the confines of a (good) social democracy that protects the most vulnerable but does not go as far as radicalising democratic structures and institutions. Depending on the restraints placed upon them – national (corruption, vested interests, etc.) or transnational (the Troika) – they can be more or less daring, but without offering a radical new vision.

The possibility of such a vision should be traced from grassroots experiments, but by no means do we have a ready blueprint. This is after all what experimentation is all about, adapted to the particularities of each framework. There is more scope for resistance, implementation of radical policies and experimentation, however, at a local level, provided that the existing governmental framework allows for that. We should not forget, for example, that the regions of Spain (the 'autonomies') are enjoying an independence that is not possible in the much more centralised Greek state. At the level of municipalities, activists can strategise local electoral victories, can implement more radical policies and can ultimately experiment with new economic initiatives. The nation state seems unable to, on the one hand, resist the worst sides of globalisation and economic liberalisation, and on the other hand, to free itself from the rigidity and lack of democracy of its institutions.

6
Europe and Its 'Peoples': Negotiating Sovereignty

Municipalism, as I argued in Chapter 5, not only has the potential to create a people that will participate actively in shaping the politics of cities and regions, but could also work as a 'laboratory' for radical experimentation, starting at the local rather than the national economic level. It seems that one of the lessons of the post-crisis period is that at the level of the nation state and electoral politics things are too rigid, too vertical, and thus incapable of allowing for the radical experimentation that a left-populist project would practice.

The politics of the nation state in turn finds expression at the supranational level, in institutions such as the European Union. If a good social democracy is better than neoliberalism or conservative protectionism at the national level, then at the supranational level a social EU is better than a neoliberal or nationalist far-right one. If we examine, for example, the politics of the Visegrád Group[1] during the increase of refugee flows during the Syrian conflict, or the 'frugal four'[2] during the EU leaders' summits on the coronavirus pandemic in July 2020, it is clear that there is a need to resist both neoliberal and far-right nationalism within the EU.

These divisions within the EU raise a number of issues in relation to European integration: the possibility of moving away from the deep-seated divisions between north and south, the persistent role of the nation state (and national interests) and the future of the union. Ultimately, for left populism it raises the question of the possibility of articulating 'a people' that will stand against the 'elites' beyond the populist right, not only at national level but also within the EU. The necessity of such a project is the necessity of international cooperation: nation states have to come together to fight global issues like global warming. There is, however, a different way of connecting transnationally. Those who emphasise that there are many political communities within a nation state (such as those in favour of municipalism, as we saw in Chapter 5) are less interested in the internationalism of the nation states and more in transnational connections bringing together localities and activists on the ground.[3]

In actual politics, however, both levels have to work together, at least for the time being. Brexit is a case in point – and one of the cases I discuss later in this chapter – because it shows that isolation or a moderate response to these questions are incapable of competing with right-wing populism at the national level and that supranational cooperation is still needed, if we aspire to connect at a more horizontalist level beyond borders. While those in favour of a 'left Brexit' would have dismissed the EU as the domain where international cooperation could enable global solutions (and that wouldn't be totally unfounded, given how national interests destroy solidarity), we have to admit that the nation state is not yet obsolete and that international cooperation is necessary. The possibility of collaboration beyond nation states and outside these institutions – what theorists call 'transnationalism' – however, seems to have only moderate effects in the contemporary set-up.

I explore the conflict between national and international sovereignty, as well as the potential for a decentralised transnationalism, by starting with the 2015 negotiations between Greece and the EU that exposed the problematic nature of current EU institutions and inspired English Euroscepticism not only for the right but also part of the left. Having said that, and arguing that rethinking the role of the nation state and transnational cooperation are vital for contemporary left populism, there is no guarantee that when a right-wing populist discourse is already deeply rooted in society it can be challenged either by a traditional left response or a left-populist one.

The Nation State and Nationalism

Let's start with the connection between the nation state and its role for left populism. In theory, left populism is very different from right populism. The latter tries to connect 'the people' with an ethnic community that is homogeneous and exclusionary. This 'us' versus 'them' mentality constructs the notion of a people around nationalism, which ultimately takes the form of 'us' – the legitimate members of the community based on some ethnic justification – opposed to those 'outside': other nations, migrants, etc. This is also the power of right-wing nationalism, as this identification of 'the people' with 'the nation' can create very strong emotional bonds.[4]

The Spanish case, and especially the case of Catalonia, has enabled members of Podemos and Catalunya en Comú to think of a different type of nationality: 'plurinationality'. The concept comes from Xavier Domènech, former member of En Comú, and it tries to address the idea of sovereignty within different levels of the nation state.[5] For those who value municipalism and see a different potential of popular sovereignty at this level, plurinationality effectively recognises that there are different political communities within the nation state.

However, let's not forget what we discussed in Chapter 5 about how Spain, with much more power in its autonomous regions, is very differently organised from the Greek centralised state. Furthermore, as in Britain, Spain's autonomous regions are advancing demands for independence, the most dramatic case being the Catalan referendum in 2017.[6]

If we subscribe to this idea of popular sovereignty at different levels beyond the nation state, we see that the idea of homogeneity within a political community is relaxed and the community itself becomes more open to accepting 'outsiders'. Barcelona, for example, although many see excessive tourism as a detriment to the identity of the city to the point that the Spanish media talks of 'turismofobia' (tourism-phobia), at the same time welcomes migrants and refugees. In June 2018 the mayor Ada Colau welcomed a rescue ship with over 600 migrants.[7]

The responses to the flows of migration towards Europe that intensified in 2015 after a number of conflicts in the Middle East, including the war in Syria, were used as ammunition by far-right parties. Migrants and refugees became scapegoats for the financial crisis, especially in countries facing the simultaneous effects of the crisis and imposed austerity while also being the first reception places for migrant and refugee flows, like Greece and Italy. According to the Dublin Regulation (which establishes which country is responsible for asylum applications under the Geneva Convention), applicants should register their interest in the first EU country they arrive in. If you move to another EU country, this second country can ask the first country to 'take you back'. It was noted as early as 2008 by the European Parliament that 'in the absence of a genuine common European asylum system and a single procedure, the Dublin system will continue to be unfair both to asylum seekers and to certain Member States'.[8] In 2015 there were 1.2 million first-time asylum applications,[9] and although Greece was not the final destination as a main point of entry it had 850,000 arrivals – creating pressure on resources even though the scapegoating of migrants by the far right was nothing but a cynical use of this situation for political gain.

The countries that received the highest number of asylum seekers had the highest disapproval rates regarding the EU's handling of the issue. The disapproval rate in Greece reached 94 per cent, even if Greece was not the final destination.[10] As migrant flows increased this reinforced hostility both towards the EU and towards the refugees themselves. The significance of the Syriza government's decision to grant nationality to second-generation immigrants in Greece, even if it mainly aimed to incorporate immigrant groups from Eastern Europe that arrived in Greece in the 1990s, is underplayed.[11] By granting non-ethnic Greeks nationality the Syriza government challenged the idea of nationhood based on ethno-cultural perceptions and advanced one of the main aims of left populism: inclusivity.

There are two further points worth noting in relation to this. First, Syriza was in power with the right-wing nationalist ANEL. This created a difficult balance in relation to the national question, even if, as many believe, ANEL proved a good partner for Syriza overall. The marriage was uncomfortable and there was occasional friction around national issues. The possibility of the coalition, however, was not a thoughtless move and it proved a successful one, supporting the case for a common front. As one Syriza journalist explained:

The possibility of a coalition government with ANEL had started before the election. There were some meetings but it was never put to the Central Committee, let alone the members [...] but we had two possibilities: either that or a minority government, something that some comrades would have preferred. But this last position would have been a mistake. There was such a fierce anti-Syriza front, even KKE ... ANEL looked quite stable in terms of its anti-memorandum beliefs, anti-corruption [...] At the end of the day, in my opinion ANEL was proven more consistent and effective and we managed to pass many bills that even the Europeans couldn't believe it. So this coalition worked for the good of the country as a whole but also for the people and the left.

This common front against the 'enemies', domestic and European, came to an end with the Prespa agreement, the 2018 agreement between Greece and the neighbouring FYROM (former Yugoslav Republic of Macedonia), resolving a long-lasting dispute over the name of the latter (which included the term 'Macedonia', also a Greek region). The difficult deal raised hopes of more, but by that point there was little support for Syriza within society and no organisational potential. As one of the Syriza interviewees explains: 'As we passed the Prespa agreement, we could have also passed the separation between state and Church. We should have done it, it was a big mistake not to. Society was more ready [than it was believed] to accept radical solutions as the Macedonian issue testifies.'

The second point is that Greek nationality (like German nationality) is defined according to the 'blood line' and one's ability to prove Greek ancestry. The policy of granting second-generation migrants citizenship was risky (electorally) but a good example of how a left-populist party can challenge the definition of political community as a 'homogeneous', exclusionary community and stand up to the nationalism of the right. To put it differently, it challenges the definition of 'the people' as *ethnos* (those of the same origin, born on the same soil) and opens up the potential of the creation of a *demos* that is more inclusive and less essentialist. Despite the Syriza bill being just a small step towards a more inclusive society, the particular policy if nothing else challenged the idea of 'the people' being equated with the nation. The same can be argued in relation to Podemos. Although some scholars focus on Errejón's attempt to articulate a national populism (the 'national-popular')[12], I try to remember that Podemos' left populism was an amalgamation of different political positions, including those more interested in movements and municipalism, like myself, all of which played an important role in establishing Barcelona en Comú for instance. Unfortunately, the Labour Party never managed to distance itself sufficiently from a discourse that scapegoated migrants, blaming them for the grievances created by neoliberal policies.

The Question of Sovereignty

During Syriza's attempts to advance a narrative against the Troika and to create a new political project that would not only get it into power but also transform existing institutions towards the creation of a radical democracy, the issue of sovereignty emerges time and again, not only in Greece but also in Spain.

Two questions emerged in relation to left populism. First, the issue of popular sovereignty and its connection vis-à-vis national sovereignty that we will examine in the next section. Second, the question of national sovereignty, which must be examined internally, as a nodal point around which we have the articulation of domestic policy (e.g. in relation to the refugee crisis in the case of Greece, or Catalan independence in Spain); and as a nodal point around which we have the articulation of foreign policy. Later I discuss the second in relation to the position of left-populist parties vis-à-vis the EU, but for the time being let's focus on nationalism in relation to left-populist strategy in terms of internal governance.

The idea of sovereignty has a long history within political philosophy and democratic theory, and there are theorists who side with national sovereignty and others with popular sovereignty. Sometimes it is a repressive device for theorists like Hobbes who dream of an all-powerful entity, the Leviathan, that will safeguard the very existence of the political community. Here sovereignty is in the hands of the state or the head of state. For other theorists sovereignty should rest with the people and only with them – in other words sovereignty is understood as popular sovereignty. What happens with populist theory? Where does sovereignty reside? Some theorists, like Hardt and Negri, accuse populist theorists like Laclau of having an idea of sovereignty as something 'outside' the people, and because of this they do not favour a project that will give real power to the people and to the grassroots. If this is the case, left populism would be a very top-down, 'vertical' project, very much in the hands of a leader or those who have the power, even if this power came from the people. This is not the case, as I have argued elsewhere,[13] and Laclau would say that the idea of sovereignty in different political projects is the outcome of more complex and less clear-cut processes.

However, sovereignty in the political discourse of the countries under examination (and within the particularity of each case) resides – or it is claimed it should reside – with the nation state. Left-populist projects either seem to follow this line, although they claim to do so in order to give power to 'the people', or seem to want to empower the people on the ground. I discuss how this idea has a particular force when related to the EU, as in the Greek case, but even if we focus within national contexts it is a difficult question for left-populist parties. Should national or popular sovereignty be prioritised, and how do the two connect? Can they talk about national sovereignty in a progressive manner or do they ultimately fall back to a regressive nationalism? And how does national sovereignty play in the international arena?

According to Óscar García Agustín, 'There is no doubt that left-wing populism targets mainly domestic politics and lacks a developed international framework.'[14] I tend to agree with this statement more in terms of theory rather than actual politics. Although the contexts are very different we should not forget how the Latin American experience of left populism created a vision, and above all structures, that bypassed nation state borders and created the transnational alliance of the Community of Latin American and Caribbean States (CELAC). The nation state is still the dominant form of identification for most people today, but its strength depends on the specific context. In some cases the context allows for more transnational forms of identification and thus the creation of a transnational people.

Left-populist parties in Greece and Spain emerged after a crisis that challenged neoliberal orthodoxy, the politics of austerity, the common frames of how debt is accumulated and the fairness of how it should be repaid. The Indignados movement in both countries is interrelated but we should not forget that this happened in a context in which the differences between Northern and Southern Europe became more prominent. On the one hand, we have divisions within the EU; on the other hand, stronger forms of identification start to develop between Southern European peoples, opening up the potential for transnational cooperation. Although the suggestion did not go further than a few discussions, some organisations of Syriza in Greece even started to contemplate either a Southern or Mediterranean alliance that could eventually break away from the rest of the EU.[15]

The suggestion may sound like wishful thinking if we think about religious, cultural and other differences, but we should not forget that the structural reforms imposed on Greece by the Troika through the memoranda have many similarities with the structural adjustments demanded by international institutions like the IMF on the Global South in the 1990s. The big difference of course is that the Greek structural adjustments were imposed for the first time, and in a visibly authoritarian manner, on a 'Western' country that is part of the 'developed' world. This is why so many people across Europe registered their dismay in the streets.

The outcome of the adjustments in South America did produce a more formalised transnational alliance and new transnational bodies. The enemy in these countries became a common enemy: US imperialism. The construction of 'a people' in South America may have started at the national level (e.g. against national oligarchies) but it was the collaboration if not submission of these oligarchies to US interests that enabled a number of countries to identify the same common enemy. We then have a transnational form of resistance that respects countries with political and economic differences, creating a transnational form of identification against the external enemy. This type of transnational way of coming together is close to what Connolly describes as 'a reciprocal virtue appropriate to a world in which partisans find themselves in intensive relations of political interdependence'.[16] These relations of interdependence and the connection between the different national demands enabled the formation of a regional bloc with broadly similar underlined goals. At the national level the left-populist approaches were quite different in terms of leadership styles and economic policy. In terms of leadership Chávez sought to forge unity while Lula attempted convergence across difference; in terms of economic policy Chávez adopted a more statist approach based on the oil reserves of Venezuela, while Lula relied more on favourable shifts in trade flows and on independent business decisions that could then enable regional projects. Despite the differences both came together in an anti-neoliberal project aiming to alleviate poverty.[17]

The Latin American case and the formation of the Bank of the South (a monetary fund and lending organisation established in 2009) is mentioned as one of the cases of cooperation between populist leaders.[18] Furthermore, these countries blocked the Free Trade Area of the Americas Agreement (FTAA) in favour of their alternative, the Bolivarian Alternative for the Peoples of Our Americas.[19] The signifier 'people' (although no one would suggest that whenever there is a reference to the people that means there is some connection with populism) here exemplifies the left-populist strategy. The founding principles of the resulting institutions are a direct challenge to neoliberal logics, and the 'us' and 'them' distinction is crystallised in their formation. Other initiatives like Petrocaribe, CELAC and UNASUR[20] make trade and investment an instrument for sustained state-regulated development, challenging the neoliberal logic of 'competition' and instead promoting the principle of 'complementarity' and 'special and differential' treatment, playing on the strengths of each country and taking into account different levels of development. The creation of a transnational 'people' is founded with respect for national sovereignty, and in this way regional integration and collective resistance to US imperialism becomes possible.

Syriza versus the EU: Setting the Table for Brexit?

On 15 July 2015, 24 hours after Greece signed an agreement in Brussels, Prime Minister Alexis Tsipras, Syriza's leader, gave an interview to the Greek public service broadcaster (ERT1).[21] Tsipras started by pledging to speak the truth, a common trope of populist leaders left and right, but also a position that if convincingly occupied expresses not only 'the truth' but also the emotional intensity that is perceived from the side of 'the people'. He continued by outlining his perception of the deal:

Yesterday, and the night before yesterday, was a bad night for Europe. It was not a night that European citizens will remember in the near future, thinking that steps were taken to return to a Europe of solidarity and democracy. The outcome of the summit and the Eurogroup was the result of immense pressure on a country and on a people who have expressed their desire democratically and tried to meet the wishes of the most economically powerful political forces in Europe. This is the truth.

This is how the negotiations were viewed by many people in Europe: an uneven battle between a weak country and the powerful; a battle that ended with an expected but still crushing defeat of the former.

It is true that some of the most common frames used by the international media included the image of Greece as the chronic patient of Europe, a metaphor that persisted while Greece was hospitalised for four years (Greece came out of the third memorandum in 2019).[22] Furthermore, the Greek people were stereotypically portrayed as 'lazy', 'frivolous' and overall responsible for their own demise. For those ideologically inclined against neoliberalism and/or the EU, however, and for those who had not benefitted from globalisation and neoliberalism over the last 40 years, the story was quite different and revealed that the EU institutions had departed from their social dimension and democratic aspiration and were not motivated by any notion of solidarity. To them, the Greek/EU negotiation crystallised the urgent need of the peoples of Europe to change this status quo either by regaining national sovereignty (advocated by both right- and left-wing Brexit projects) or by entertaining the possibility of transnational populist reform (through projects similar to DiEM25).

From Tsipras' perspective, at that point there were three options for Greece and his government: bankruptcy and an exit from the euro, accepting an agreement (with all the structural adjustments and austerity) or a third option favoured by Wolfgang Schäuble, the German minister of finance, who adopted the hardest line with Southern European countries hit by the crisis – a eurozone with a core and a periphery, that is, a 'two-speed eurozone'.[23]

We should also not forget that Greece had capital controls from June 2015, after the decision of the ECB to stop liquidity to the Greek banks, a decision very similar to those affecting Argentina during the crisis of 2001. Tsipras (and a good part of the Greek people, who voted for him for a second time in September 2015) took the second option. Other members of Syriza believed that, unable to follow its programme, Syriza should have resigned from power. Finally, another part of Syriza believed that Tsipras should have refused a deal, even if that meant an exit from the eurozone (gaining monetary sovereignty) and potentially the EU. We will never have an answer to the 'what if' question, but for most it was clear that the majority of members within Syriza never had and never would have chosen the third option.

The break with those espousing the third option came just before the September 2015 election (an election which was necessary since the manifesto on which Syriza was elected in January 2015 was not valid anymore).

In the years that followed the Syriza government's tone regarding the negotiations changed, contrasting the results with the memorandum of the pre-2015 New Democracy and PASOK (Samaras–Venizelos) government, and in a way presenting the July 2015 deal as a success. The demand by the Troika for primary surpluses was described by Prime Minister Tsipras in the middle of his term as follows:

> The central point of the negotiation was the reduction of primary surpluses, which would ensure the necessary fiscal space for the Greek economy. The previous Samaras–Venizelou agreement set 3% surplus targets for 2015, 4.5% for 2016, 4.5% for 2017 and 4.2% for 2018. In addition, the infamous success story had left behind it another budget gap of approximately two billion euros, which needed new measures to be filled, as the ND [New Democracy]-PASOK government did not achieve the target of a 1.5% primary surplus in 2014. On the contrary, the agreement of July 2015 sets as goals -0.25% for 2015, 0.5% for 2016, 1.75% for 2017 and 3.5% for 2018. This means that 20 billion euros will remain in the real economy, in society, during these four years, instead of fuelling the irrational measures that would be required to fulfil the goals of the previous agreement between ND and PASOK.[24]

Although this may very well have been the case, the hardship on the ground (with continued unemployment, heavy taxation for the middle classes and cuts for pensioners, to name a few of the continuous grievances of the Greek people) meant that any boasting was perceived as 'arrogance', something the Syriza government paid the price for in the 2019 election.

Obviously this was not the only factor for the defeat of Syriza in 2019 and we should also look at the transformation of the right-wing position. After the first victory of Syriza in January 2015, Cas Mudde, a well-known scholar of populism (though one who understands populism very differently and less sympathetically than I do) made some predictions which, although not wrong per se, missed the importance of Syriza's victory as well as its subsequent defeat. He claimed that the right wing in Greece remained dominated by New Democracy without serious contestation from the far-right parties like Golden Dawn. What happened, however, with New Democracy is that it progressively absorbed part of the far right, in a similar manner to the Conservatives in Britain under Boris Johnson, dropping the façade of liberal conservatism. Mudde is of course one of the people that often talks about the 'far left' and the 'far right' in one breath. Although he argued that the EU will not move to the 'far left', in hindsight we know that the EU is changing – not because it moved to the left, but because countries like Britain moved to the populist, Eurosceptic right.[25] What is soothing for a centrist like Mudde, and for the traditional left, is the confirmation that the EU is an unreformable 'capitalist club' set to continue with the same institutions. But for those inspired by left populism the period after the crisis marks a missed opportunity to create an EU for its people.

Nation State(s), National Sovereignty and Brexit

The Syriza negotiations threw a different light on the idea of international cooperation and solidarity across Europe. One of the key issues within the debates over the role of the EU has to do with the role of the nation state and how it connects with visions of Europe. Generally speaking, when we discuss the nation state the general assumption is that we refer to the main organising unit of society. The nation itself is a constructed or 'imagined' community that came into being at the beginning of the Industrial Revolution, with the advent of communications, transport, etc., enabling different people to think of themselves as one.[26] The state refers to the political structure and governance of this community. In terms of the British state, it is traditionally thought of in non-interventionist terms due to the tradition of English liberalism, and as a result Britain has seen Europe as a free market project rather than a political project. This can be contrasted with the Danish state (which joined the EU in 1973, the same time as the UK), for example, where the state is also understood in terms of the 'welfare state'. The political outcome is that in the case of the Danish state there is a certain sensitivity about the EU straying into certain areas, a concern that in the past came mainly from the left. The Danish side may have been in favour of the free market too, but at the same time it wanted guarantees for the protection of workers' safety, for example.[27]

One of the main 'nodes' around which the Brexit debate centred relates to European governance. There are a number of positions that have been part of the British discourse, the most dominant being the 'liberal economic community' and its social democratic sister, the 'social democratic economic community'. The first, dominant from the 1970s onwards, was legitimised on the basis of economic output and could be seen as aiming to promote Thatcherism on a European scale. The latter, also restricting the European project to the economic sphere, was legitimised on the basis of the participation of governments and became dominant within the New Labour government. Associated with the 'third way', it still legitimises neoliberal economic hegemony but gives it a more 'social' face.[28]

What is important is that both positions focus on the maximum economic output that could be achieved through the union, and there is a clear divide between politics and economics. When the Thatcher government favoured a strengthening of the European Court of Justice (ECJ) in the Single European Act, it was effectively saying that economic governance is not about politics, and government interference has to be limited. According to this logic, the ECJ could provide the legal expertise to settle any disputes. This was enough and no further reflection on economic governance was needed.[29]

Within the context of the liberal economic framework (dominant, as I said, in Thatcherism), however, there is a question about who occupied centre stage: the answer is the individual consumer and entrepreneur rather than the citizen and by extension parliaments.[30] When the citizen is put in second place, has little consumer power and starts to perceive entrepreneurialism as a myth, the question about who should be put centre stage at the national and supranational level re-emerges.

This is the moment for the populist right, in the case of the UK and Boris Johnson. What he managed to do successfully was to make the EU the target of all grievances associated with neoliberalism. The success was down to displacing the problem not only in economic terms (which may lack some affective power in the political discourse) but also anchoring it around 'Englishness', or the demise of it. Remember that throughout his involvement with Brexit the Irish issue was downplayed, only to return with a vengeance not only as one of the main sticking points of the Withdrawal Agreement but also the deal negotiations. The position of Ireland and Scotland seemed secondary in his narrative which was doing exactly that: putting Englishness at the centre of any demand.

One of the key arguments in favour of Brexit for Boris Johnson was the reclaiming of national sovereignty vis-à-vis the EU institutions. Throughout the Brexit saga, any political actor seen to question the decision of the referendum was seen as an enemy of 'the people' and branded undemocratic. This very successful right-wing populist division soon took the form of the people versus parliament and enabled the prime minister to make unprecedented moves. In a very successful narrative, national sovereignty was equated with popular sovereignty and anyone deemed as inhibiting the former was automatically against the latter – against the power of the people.

In August 2019 Johnson enacted the prorogation of the British Parliament (that is, its suspension) for five weeks in the run-up to the 31 October Brexit deadline, in order to avoid scrutiny of his plans. The decision was found unlawful by the UK's Supreme Court in September 2019. Supreme Court President Judge Lady Hale emphasised that Johnson's decision to advise the Queen to suspend Parliament 'had the effect of frustrating or preventing the ability of Parliament to carry out its constitutional functions without reasonable justification'.[31] The role of Parliament in what was portrayed as delaying or even suspending the 'will of the people', and the regaining of national sovereignty, was not incompatible with the creation of an enemy which was first used at the national level against the British Parliament and then extended to the supranational level.

The Brexit narrative was anchored around the undemocratic character of the EU institutions and was repeated by both right- and left-wing Brexiteers. Although the latter had a point in that democracy within the EU was problematic and subordinated to the economic interests of the powerful nations within the EU, themselves subordinated to the neoliberal paradigm, there was little debate over the actual representational structures and their adequacy for transnational politics. The debates – hundreds of debates where I myself made the case for remaining an EU member, even if reluctantly – seemed blind to processes like the European Parliament elections and the Council of Ministers, made up of government ministers from every member state. The European Commission, a non-elected body, is the executive branch and at least in theory accountable to the European Parliament.

The debate conflated (very successfully for the Brexit side) two separate issues, democracy and representation. To put it differently, the British Parliament is elected and represents the people (at least those who have the right to vote). How democratic it is is a different question. The 'first-past-the-post' system has been widely criticised and calls for some form of proportional representation have been part of the political agenda for years. Not to mention that any nation state whose head is established by hereditary rights is already quite far from 'true' democracy, let alone being ruled by the people. From the start the story of Brexit is full of violations of parliamentary democracy in the name of national sovereignty. The EU Withdrawal Act of 2018, the law that repeals the European Communities Act of 1972 thus nullifying EU law, gave ministers what have been called 'Henry VIII powers' to make changes to legislation with less parliamentary scrutiny.

Similarly, while both former Conservative prime ministers David Cameron and Theresa May hadn't been against the state aid rules of the EU (which after all are very neoliberal, blocking the interference of the state in saving or helping ailing sectors), Johnson made state aid a point of contention in his EU negotiations in 2020. In his narrative it was connected with the issue of sovereignty, but it could also be a calculated move as EU rules block aid towards companies his particular government would like to assist. When this was an issue in August 2020, the General Court annulled the decision of the European Commission (2016) ordering Ireland to recover back-taxes from Apple that the commission considered to be illegal state aid.[32] Even if this decision were to work in favour of the UK's potential plans to assist particular multinationals, the EU's competition policy could be an impediment. We should not forget that the United Kingdom had previously blocked the commission's proposal of a financial transaction tax[33] and it has pushed the neoliberal agenda throughout its membership. The Common Market was Thatcher's child, after all.

The Brexit trajectory is full of instances like this, but it did manage to capitalise on conflating the existence of representational structures versus the real democratic character of these structures, and constructing as an 'enemy' of Brexit anyone scrutinising either the process or the legal manifestation of the exit, both domestically and at EU level.

We can observe here the power of the populist Brexit discourse. There were many proposals on the other side of the debate of course, such as one signed by Thomas Piketty, the French economist who recognised the tension between national sovereignty and EU institutions but also the possibility of reforming the treaties (something most Brexiteers would reject). He and his co-signatories contended that, especially in an era of globalised financial capitalism, the need to regulate the economy was paramount. The greater involvement of nation states could be the creation of a 'European chamber' involving the countries of the eurozone, which would enable more democracy and would, as it happens, be a step towards European integration.[34]

The same strategy was used to create an enemy of anyone examining the particular form Brexit could take. By giving primacy to national sovereignty, the question of popular sovereignty – the question of the long-term benefits for the people (British people, since EU nationals were not given the right to vote in the referendum) – was bypassed and the mere posing of the question was immediately positioning those who were less 'patriotic' as being in the 'enemy camp'. Take for example new trade deals, which the Johnson government pushed as a manifestation of the freedom the UK would enjoy in making its own bilateral deals all around the world without being burdened by EU bureaucracy. However, the UK government also made sure that neither the public nor the opposition would be in a position to scrutinise any trade negotiations. The outcome of these negotiations could potentially place the United Kingdom but above all the British people at the mercy of big corporations.

Nick Dearden, director of campaign group Global Justice Now, reflected on how Jeremy Corbyn, as leader of the opposition, went head-to-head with Boris Johnson on national TV on 19 November 2019 with a pile of almost entirely blacked-out papers in front of him: the only published details of the trade deals discussed with the US government. These were the same papers that had also been blacked out when their release was demanded by NGOs, blocking both parliament and society from having a say. Eventually the unredacted papers were leaked on discussion website Reddit.[35]

Apart from the lack of democratic accountability and even a minimum of transparency, trade deals of the type that Johnson envisioned with the US (similar to the Transatlantic Trade and Investment Partnership) have a number of provisions that undermine democracy. One of these is the famous 'corporate courts' of the Investor–State Dispute Settlement (ISDS), giving the power to international investors to sue states that pass legislation deemed harmful to their profits. If anything could undermine national sovereignty it would be this type of deal.

However, because Brexit remained empty of any particular content for as long as possible, even the issue of what type of deal would define the relationship with the EU (or even whether there would be a deal at all) remained unclear. While Theresa May tried to shape a deal that was close to the Norwegian model, thus favouring a soft Brexit with less negative economic impact but positioning the UK as a 'rule taker', Boris Johnson moved further by referencing the Canadian Comprehensive Economic and Trade Agreement (which had been fiercely contested across Europe and amended) and even an Australian deal that wasn't in place in 2020.

The relationship between the UK and the EU has always been a contentious issue within British politics. The first referendum on whether or not the relationship with the Common Market should be continued (Britain had joined the European Common Market in 1973) took place in 1975, with 67 per cent voting to remain. Despite Eurosceptic voices within the Labour Party, the Labour governments also focused on the economic output argument, though it did bring in the social dimension though justice and employment for example, and Labour did try to strengthen the importance of both the European Parliament and of national parliaments in European policy making.[36]

The Brexit referendum, however, was largely a product of the ruling Conservative Party, based not on the need to rethink the EU (which the Labour Party under Corbyn would have had a lot to say about) but the product of two intertwined factors: first, the rise of UKIP, led at that point by Nigel Farage, which could have presented an electoral threat to the Conservatives in some areas; and second, internal divisions within the Tories over their relationship with the EU. As a result, then Prime Minister David Cameron – in order to solidify his leadership and election – promised a referendum (legally not binding) which eventually took place on 23 June 2016, resulting in 51.9 per cent of the vote being cast in favour of leaving the EU. Cameron, who had joined the 'in' campaign Britain Stronger in Europe, was forced to resign and was succeeded by Theresa May in July 2016. The leadership of Theresa May, which favoured a softer Brexit and was closer to the Thatcherite position emphasising the economic benefits of the EU, remained fragile due to Brexit. When the withdrawal agreement was ultimately approved by the British Parliament in January 2020, after being rejected three times, Theresa May had already resigned and been succeeded by Boris Johnson. We could argue that the basis of the narrative opening the road to Boris Johnson had been set by May herself: she encouraged nationalism and the scapegoating of migrants (especially those of the Eastern bloc) as the reason for poverty and unemployment in the north of England. From Cameron's economic neoliberalism and globalism to May's neoliberalism with elements of national protectionism and social conservatism, both leaders paved the way for Johnson's right-wing populism where nationalism, xenophobia, Islamophobia and anti-migration, combined with a neoliberal agenda, played a central role.

The Labour Party, anxious not to become 'the enemy of the people', voted in favour of triggering Article 50 (the article setting in motion the Brexit process) in 2017, with 47 voting against, unable to change the narrative that was already set in motion. If it didn't contribute to xenophobia and nationalism (and many say it did), Labour's lukewarm position following the right-wing discourse didn't help either.

The Labour Party failed to adopt a clear policy regarding Brexit for far too long. Knowing that the referendum had created a big divide in society, Corbyn adopted a policy of 'constructive ambiguity' while different factions within the party were pulling in different directions. In 2017, while addressing a meeting of *Chartist* magazine on Brexit, someone whispered to me that Jon Lansman – founder of pro-Corbyn pressure group Momentum – had messaged Momentum delegates at the Labour conference that Brexit should not be prioritised, in effect meaning it should not be put up for a vote. This is indicative of how for years the Brexit issue was avoided by the Labour Party – not unreasonably, but in a way that was completely inadequate given the political capital at stake regarding Brexit.

Party policy only changed at the party conference in September 2018, when 150 CLPs passed a motion against Brexit and in favour of leaving open the option of a 'public vote' (an attempt to avoid the toxic term 'second referendum', implying the annulment of the first). At a six-hour composite meeting deciding on the final text that would be put to conference, a point of contestation was whether the possibility of remaining in the EU would be an option for the popular vote. The meeting ended with this choice being left open and was confirmed by the conference vote. Although the adoption of this policy was seen as being responsible for the demise of the party at the 2019 election, it was also down to the fact that a large part of the party base was in favour of Remain, even if some reluctantly. At the next conference in 2019 the motion (number 13) for active campaigning in favour of Remain was rejected amid confusion, while the next motion (number 14) approved a referendum on the deal brought to parliament by the Tories. In other words, while the possibility of a referendum was approved, the position the party would take at such an eventuality was rejected.[37] For a number of commentators this attempt to appeal to both Remain and Leave voters was extremely risky, and in the event it cost Corbyn the next election.

It is true that in 2018, when version after version of the withdrawal agreement had been rejected, some, including Shadow Chancellor John McDonnell, flirted with the idea of a second referendum on the basis that there was an impasse, and since Labour could not support a general election at that moment it could be a way out. On 23 June 2018, the two-year anniversary of the referendum, 100,000 people marched in favour of remaining in the EU. The 'People's Vote' march drew participants from across the political spectrum with speakers including David Lammy (Labour), Caroline Lucas (Greens), Vince Cable (Liberal Democrats) and Anna Soubry (Conservative).

This was an attempt to create a different equivalence chain (in favour of Remain) connecting a multiplicity of demands. It was doomed to fail, however, and this is another interesting point for left populism: bringing demands together and creating a chain cannot expand indefinitely. If it expands too much, bringing almost everyone in, it becomes less convincing and I think this was a big problem for the People's Vote. Any left-populist strategy, dividing the political field into two camps and fighting against the Conservatives' Brexit from that perspective, needed to be an initiative led by Corbyn. But this never happened.

The most concrete proposal from the Labour side seemed to come from Keir Starmer (then shadow Brexit minister) with his 'six tests', setting a more coherent though not very inspiring position for Labour.[38] Fast forward two years and a few months before the end of the transition period in December 2020, the logic of the Labour Party remains the same and Keir Starmer now demands from Boris Johnson's government that it should keep its own promise to 'get Brexit done'. The tactical logic behind that is that for Starmer, now the leader of the Labour Party, he needs to show he accepts Brexit in order to win back parliamentary seats that were allegedly lost because of the Labour Party's stance, and emphasise the government's incompetence instead.[39] With the completion of Brexit at the end of 2020 (and the admittedly bad trade deal that was secured at the eleventh hour) Starmer started to focus on the competence of the Conservative government (on Brexit but also the COVID pandemic) rather than offering any radical transformative narrative.

From International Cooperation to Transnationalism

In 2015 Yanis Varoufakis, together with other well-known personalities of the left like Jean-Luc Mélenchon (co-president of the French Left Party and in 2016 founder of 'Unbowed France'), launched 'Plan B' which in the 2019 European Parliament elections became the alliance 'Now the People'. Plan B is interesting, first of all because it brought very different personalities and claims to a left-populist style of politics together into an attempt at international cooperation. On the one hand we have Mélenchon, openly hostile to Syriza and calling for the party's expulsion from the European left party for caving in to the Troika-imposed austerity policies. The suggestion was seen as divisive by Syriza[40] and was not adopted (in pragmatic terms, Syriza is the only party of the European left that has been the winner of a national election), though the demand is not unfounded since Syriza has often worked more closely with the Socialists and Democrats group in the European Parliament. Furthermore, Mélenchon has an anti-EU position that is at odds with other groups in the alliance. I am not aware of what Mélenchon's feelings were in 2019 after Pablo

Iglesias formed a government with PSOE, but I don't think this would be their only point of tension. Mélenchon has instrumentalised left populism in a particular manner that is quite nation focused, in some cases expressing ambiguous anti-migrant positions that are common in the right-wing populist discourse and not unfamiliar to certain parts of the left, especially when confronted by strong far-right, anti-migrant opponents.[41] The Labour Party itself is not a stranger to such positions, especially pre-Corbyn. The affinity between Mélenchon's discourse and Labour came together in a packed event of the World Transformed (a Momentum-inspired festival) in 2018 when Mélenchon declared that he didn't want to interfere in the Brexit debate – before letting the audience know he was in favour of Brexit.

Another of Mélenchon's temporary allies in the attempt at international cooperation was Yanis Varoufakis. After all, as an interviewee, said to me:

> Varoufakis is the first one who said very early that if you owe someone money, that person has also a problem, not only you. Our economists didn't understand that […] In the process however this advantage got lost because they shield themselves. At that point we should have changed our strategy a bit […] What Varoufakis should have realised earlier on is that it didn't have as much clout as he thought, the fact that they would also have a problem is overstated. They wouldn't. Look, here they don't even have a big problem with Brexit. It will have a negative effect in the long run but this is different.

Varoufakis inspired resistance to EU institutions but soon created his own project, DiEM25, an attempt to create a European people(s) that would demand reform of the EU. He never associated with populism himself, despite the textbook attempt to create (from the top) a populist divide. He said: 'We are here to bury populism. A populism that … the Greek people remember, the PASOK under Simitis, a time when the biggest debt bubble in the Eurozone both public and private was building up, while the Greek people were being told they belonged to the hardcore of the Eurozone.'[42]

Varoufakis was seen as one 'speaking the truth' to the people of Europe, an important trope within populism and used by Tsipras himself as we saw earlier.[43] Despite DiEM25 claiming to be inspired by the Indignados movement, however, and aspiring to be one if we go by the term in the name (Democracy in Europe Movement 2025), a striking starting point for DiEM25 was that it failed to connect with existing movements, as for example John Malamatinas from Blockupy states in an open letter to Varoufakis, leading to the conclusion that DiEM25 was 'more efficient in being involved in social struggles rather than connecting them as part of a common movement'.[44] Despite the relative gains of DiEM25, it seems to be a transnational populist project like the one envisioned by this book that I believe is still to come.

For the time being, international cooperation within the institutions of the EU will continue. However, what DiEM25 showed is that the possibility for a left-populist project is open and it is worth challenging international institutions. For this to be possible, however, as has been the case for national left-populist projects, it should be based on existing movements aiming at more horizontalist ties between communities beyond the nation state. Brexit was a missed opportunity for a left-leaning Labour Party to challenge EU institutions from within. But the articulation of the popular will, as I said earlier, depends on a correlation of forces that in the UK led to a right-wing, populist project like Brexit. The latter entailed a promise (even if unfounded) of a better future that could unite the long-standing grievances of the British people. In effect, what the Johnson government did throughout the referendum and the negotiations with the EU was to reinvent the rules of the game, or what we earlier called transversality.

Conclusion: Where We Are Today with Left Populism

Since the financial crisis of 2008 and the subsequent rise of left parties with 'populist' elements – in the sense that they were dividing the political space between an 'us' (the people) and 'them' (the enemy) – many things have changed. In Greece Syriza lost the 2019 general election and was succeeded by a right-wing government led by Kyriakos Mitsotakis, a member of a political dynasty started by the late Konstantinos Mitsotakis, his father and prime minister between 1990 to 1993.

When Kyriakos Mitsotakis won the 2019 election Greece had already left the third memorandum[1] in August 2018, and according to the leader of Syriza, Alexis Tsipras, his government had left the state budget with a surplus of 37 billion euros, a 'safety cushion' as he characteristically said.[2] A few months into the new right-wing government the Covid-19 pandemic brought the Greek economy to a standstill. The Mitsotakis government imposed strict lockdown rules from the start and the first wave of the pandemic left Greece unscarred. One of the first economic scandals associated with the pandemic was the payment to a number of media outlets of 20 million euros to broadcast the campaigns 'we stay home' and 'we stay safe'. The campaigns (which in most other European countries would have been aired for free) became an excuse to subsidise government-friendly media without any objective criteria for their selection. 'Petsas' list', named after the government's media representative, allocated less than 1 per cent of the budget to opposition media.[3] It also allegedly subsidised media that promoted anti-mask conspiracy theories.[4]

The spending of public money for the benefit of the government's friends and the increase to the defence budget, after provocations from Turkey in summer 2020, will no doubt contribute to the dire situation Greece will find itself in the proceeding years. With the increase in coronavirus cases and the sharp increase in deaths after the relaxation of the initial measures in order to assist the Greek economy and its overreliance on tourism, with disappointing results (revenue 83 per cent lower than in 2019)[5], the policy is to keep fatalities to a minimum in a country where the national health service had crumpled under the pressures of the 2008 crisis and the government is keen to subsidise private medical interests.[6]

During this new crisis the left and especially Syriza do not seem to win any support on the ground, although it is exactly the time for a left populism that will put the lives of the people above the economy, opening up the discussion of redistribution and state support. Like in Britain, right-wing governments have offered some support packages but they are not even close to what is needed to create some real security.

For many the 31.5 per cent of the vote that Syriza got in the 2019 election signalled that Syriza had to form a broad progressive front, and the transformation of the party was well underway in 2020. The transformation of the party is recognised by Tsipras: 'Syriza of 2004 was not the same as Syriza in 2015, nor is Syriza of 2015 with Syriza – Progressive Alliance of 2020. Because parties to a large extent – and because of the crisis of the party model – prefer to reflect the base of their voters. Not only their members.'[7] When Syriza included 'progressive alliance' in its name in September 2020, it was coupled with a renewed attempt to attract members since the local branches had been closed since 2015 and many members had left or were inactive. Visually the new name found expression in the five-pointed star, each according to Tsipras symbolising ideals not only of the left but more broadly of the democratic forces: democracy, solidarity, justice, freedom and equality. Answering questions as to whether Syriza is turning into another PASOK, thus becoming one of the two partners (the other being New Democracy) sharing in the same systemic game, the leader of Syriza denied this was the case, arguing that it will not 'compromise on the role of administrator and seeks an alternative governmental path for the benefit of the social majority, without dogmatism and entanglements'.[8]

That sounded good in theory, but in reality this latest turn fuelled new antagonisms within the party with many long-term members expressing reservations if not direct objections. Some point to the paradox that on the one hand the leader of Syriza seems to believe with the rest of the radical left that in the time of neoliberalism the conditions for a radical movement are ripe although the left fails to take over; on the other hand, when discussing the Greek situation he adopts a centre-left logic. In other words, while Tsipras accepts that at the international level the people(s) are radicalised, in the Greek case he argues for the need to express the centre or what he calls the 'democratic constituency'. There is a huge difference, however, between moving to the centre in order to become (or remain) electorally successful (something that many parties did in the past in order to 'catch all' the voters) and trying to express the broad progressive constituency (which should have been radicalised after the financial crisis of 2008) by putting forward a radical programme; in other words, expressing their radicalisation at an electoral level. This ambivalence is important in assessing the potential of left populism as a radical strategy.

On the ground, despite renewed rhetoric by Syriza about the need for enlarging its membership and enabling members' participation, there is not much going on, either at the level of the party or in terms of broader social movements – apart from the student movement, which has had a revival after continuous attacks by the right-wing government. In November 2019 hundreds of young Greeks occupied the Economic University of Athens, with widespread mobilisations across Greece. What was at stake was the abolition of 'university asylum', the 1982 bill that protects freedom of expression within universities. Targeting the young, in an attempt to silence the most vocal critics, continued with raids on bars and clubs, with methods that violated civil liberties in the most profound ways.[9] Student mobilisations continued during the pandemic with many schools being occupied, demanding the implementation of safety protocols at schools (especially minimising the number of students in each classroom).

In Britain a leadership contest after the 2019 general election put Keir Starmer at the head of the Labour Party, much to the discontent of part of the left which saw a return to centre politics (if not the right). Although it is true that Starmer's leadership was expected to be very different from that of Jeremy Corbyn, for the left a number of questions arose regarding why Corbyn's star declined within the party as well as questions over why a much awaited electoral victory was not delivered (especially during the 2017 election when the dynamics were in Labour's favour). A number of explanations have been offered: for some it was the unclear position of the party on Brexit, for others the antisemitism scandals and the inability of Corbyn to present a 'patriotic' profile, especially around issues of foreign policy. They all agreed that the attacks launched on him from the right of the party and the relentless smearing by the mainstream media also contributed significantly, although this was to be expected. The question is, as always, was there a different strategy that could have counteracted these attacks? My answer is positive but it would demand a closer engagement with and acceptance of a left-populist strategy.

We should not forget, however, that political terrain is shaped by both sides and in Britain Corbyn had to face the populist right wing (Boris Johnson) which proved much better equipped to rally 'a people' in support of some policies that could significantly hurt established rights and the power of the people to intervene in political processes. An example could be the new trade deals after Brexit which could potentially support ISDS courts in giving businesses the right to sue the state if their interests are curbed.

A section of Corbyn's supporters was not yet ready to reflect on the strategy of the former leader. Instead they found themselves embroiled in another intra-party struggle. Starmer tried early on to differentiate his leadership from his predecessor, signalling this shift with the slogan 'Under New Management' and later 'A New Leadership'. Strategists pointed to how the former was a bit too backward-looking, although I believe the main problem was the reference to a type of politics that does not inspire and does the opposite of creating a populist hype. How much Starmer will live up to the 'new leadership' label remains to be seen. For a long period during the pandemic it seemed to have chosen a very different strategy, one that sits on the fence letting the opponent burn whatever political capital they may have.

As with the case of Syriza in Greece, however, the left-leaning Corbynite Labour – the more traditional, lexit side of it – was defeated not only electorally but also by losing power within important organisations like Momentum (which in January 2020 balloted its members on whether to back up Rebecca Long-Bailey, Corbyn's chosen candidate, offering no other alternative)[10] by left slates critical of some of Corbyn's policies like Brexit, pitching 'anti-continuity' and vowing to democratise the organisation.[11] It is interesting that the opposition slate emphasised 'working-class' politics, which as we have discussed is sometimes perceived as a rival strategy to 'populism'.

Spain, on the other hand, seems to be doing better than both Greece and Britain politically, although it has been hit hard by the pandemic. One of the latest measures announced by the Unidas Podemos/PSOE government is an increase in corporate tax, wealth tax and personal income tax for large fortunes and companies.[12] It seems that the coalition between the two parties works, and by doing so it poses an important question: are the impediments faced by the populist left ameliorated when in power with an established social democratic party (even if this means going to bed with those who were 'the enemy' in 2015)? After all, there is little evidence in the discussion in this book that left-populist parties fared any better in terms of radical policies when in government. Furthermore, we should not forget that Pablo Iglesias adopted a mixed, even ambiguous strategy to get to that place. On the one hand, he 'stole' the insight of his once second in command, Íñigo Errejón, who much earlier on advocated a collaboration with PSOE and who was the one more committed to a left populism. On the other hand, by bringing Podemos and IU together, he dragged a more traditional left party (IU) into this collaboration. In other words, Errejón's strategy worked (for Iglesias) with the added bonus of engaging other parts of the left as well. One of course cannot avoid wondering what would have happened if that had taken place some years earlier, not only for Spain but also in relation to the EU's political direction.

From National to Supranational Politics

As the world finds itself in an unprecedented health crisis that no doubt will be followed by an economic recession, a left-populist strategy should be considered as a way of withstanding the far-right populist wave that in late 2020 is already working within the anti-mask conspiracy movement and the 'libertarian' politics of Trump and Johnson. International collaboration and the possibility of a trans-nationalist populist project seems quite plausible in the face of a global pandemic and predicted recession. Syriza's leader, Alexis Tsipras, had an optimistic outlook regarding the direction of world politics:

Strange as it may seem to you what I will tell you, … things in the world seem to be moving to the left and to more radical policies. Precisely because neoliberal capitalism can no longer provide answers to the current conditions of the multidimensional crisis. In the United States, for example, Democrats chose Biden because they did not believe Sanders could defeat Trump, but their base seems to want anyone who defeats Trump to follow Sanders' policies.[13]

Although this optimism has still to manifest itself in a concrete way, we cannot fail to recognise that transnational solidarity and cooperation is crucial. If anything the pandemic is urging us to do so. On the other hand, we have supranational institutions like the EU that seem to lack the will to embrace a more radical vision and member states that seem to determine their position based on their particular national interests. A transnational left-populist project could be the way to bring about change, equality and solidarity even at the eleventh hour.

Notes

Introduction

1. Burns, A. and Corasaniti, N. 2016. 'Donald Trump Assails His Accusers as Liars, and Unattractive'. *New York Times*. Available at: www.nytimes.com/2016/10/15/us/politics/donald-trump-campaign.html (accessed 20 November 2020).

2. See Tormey, S. 2019. *Populism*. Oneworld, chapter 4.

3. *The Independent*. 2020. 'Boris Johnson Calls for Legal Change to "Send Away" More Asylum Seekers Amid Surge in Migrant Boats'. Available at: www.independent.co.uk/news/uk/home-news/migrant-crossings-channel-france-border-ministry-defence-home-office-a9662536.html (accessed 20 November 2020).

4. Formerly called Unidos Podemos.

5. www.euractiv.com. 2020. 'Spain Unveils "Unprecedented" €200 Billion Coronavirus Package'. Available at: www.euractiv.com/section/economy-jobs/news/spain-unveils-unprecedented-e200-billion-coronavirus-package/ (accessed 20 November 2020).

6. Carreño, B. 2020. 'Honeymoon Over: Spain's Fragile Coalition Tested by Pandemic Politics'. Available at: https://uk.reuters.com/article/us-health-coronavirus-spain-politics/honeymoon-over-spains-fragile-coalition-tested-by-pandemic-politics-idUKKCN2262C4 (accessed 20 November 2020).

7. Since the beginning of the crisis I have conducted about 50 semi-structured interviews with activists and this work informed papers and book chapters including: Prentoulis, M. and Thomassen, L. 2013. 'Political Theory in the Square: Protest, Representation and Subjectification'. *Contemporary Political Theory*, 12(3), pp. 166–84 and Prentoulis, M. and Kyriakidou, M. 2019. 'Media and Collective Action in Greece: From Indignation to Solidarity'. *International Journal of Communication*, 13, pp. 22–40. All interviews have been anonymised.

8. I conducted about 20 interviews with party officials and journalists from Syriza, Podemos and Labour over the period 2012–19 and I hope I will use them more systematically in the future. All interviews have been anonymised.

Chapter 1

1. See Friedan, B. 1963. *The Feminine Mystique*. Norton.

2. For the different types of political representation, see H. Pitkin's seminal 1972 work, *The Concept of Representation*. University of California Press.

3. For a theoretical discussion on representation in Laclau's populist theory see Thomassen, L. 2019. 'Representing the People: Laclau as a Theorist of Representation'. *New Political Science*, 41(2), pp. 329–44.

4. Grattan, L. 2016. *Populism in Power: Radical Grassroots Democracy in America*. Oxford University Press, p. 4

5. Mouffe, C. 2018. *For a Left Populism*. Verso, p. 60.

6. Müller, J.-W. 2017. *What Is Populism?* Penguin, p. 27.

7. Müller, *What Is Populism?*, 29.

8. Laclau, E. 2005. *On Populist Reason*. Verso, pp. 162–3.

9. According to some sources the terms 'identity politics' was first introduced in a 1977 statement by the black feminist group the Combahee River Collective and referred to the experience of oppression, injustice and exclusion felt by social groups like women and ethnic and sexual minorities.

10. A quite abstract discussion on 'contingency' can be found in Butler J., Laclau, E. and Žižek, S. 2000. *Contingency, Hegemony, Universality*. Verso. The discussion here draws from Laclau, E. 2000. 'Identity and Hegemony: The Role of Universality in the Constitution of Political Logics', in Laclau et al. *Contingency, Hegemony, Universality*, pp. 44–89.

11. Laclau, E. and Mouffe, C. 1985. *Hegemony and Socialist Strategy*. Verso, p. 105.

12. See Laclau and Mouffe, *Hegemony and Socialist Strategy*, pp. 96–8.

13. See articles in the left-wing *Jacobin* magazine, e.g. Heideman, P. 2020. 'Class Rules Everything Around Me'. Available at: https://jacobinmag. com/2019/05/working-class-structure-oppression-capitalist-identity (accessed 23 November 2020). The magazine has hosted some very interesting and telling debates on the issue.

14. Mouffe, *For a Left Populism*, pp. 66–8.

15. Tony Blair says the Tories and Labour engaged in 'populism running riot'. *The Guardian*, 25 November 19. Available at: www.theguardian. com/politics/2019/nov/25/tony-blair-tories-labour-populism-election; www.theguardian.com/politics/video/2019/nov/25/tony-blair-says-conservatives-and-labour-are-peddling-fantasies-video (accessed 28 November 2019).

16. Crouch, C. 2010. *Post-democracy*, Polity Press.

17. Crouch, *Post-democracy*, p. 4.

18. Some of the early discussions on these issues can be found in Franklin, B. 2004. *Packaging Politics*. Arnold; and McNair, B. 1995. *Introduction to Political Communication*, Routledge.

19. Manin, B. 1997. *The Principles of Representative Government*. Cambridge University Press.

20. Franze, J. 2018. 'The Podemos Discourse: A Journey from Antagonism to Agonism', in García Agustín, Ó. and Briziarelli, M. (eds) *Podemos and*

the New Political Cycle: Left-Wing Populism and Anti-establishment Politics. Palgrave Macmillan.

21. Mudde, C. 2018. 'How Populism became the Concept that Defines Our Age'. *The Guardian*, 22 November 2018. Available at: www.theguardian. com/commentisfree/2018/nov/22/populism-concept-defines-our-age (accessed 25 April 2019).

22. Mudde, C. and Kaltwasser, R.C. 2017. *Populism: A Very Short Introduction.* Oxford University Press; Mudde, C. 2017. 'Populism Isn't Dead: Here Are Five Things You Need to Know about It'. *The Guardian*, 7 July 2017. Available at: www.theguardian.com/commentisfree/2017/jul/07/ populism-dead-european-victories-centrists (accessed 23 November 2020).

23. Freeden, M. 1996 *Ideologies and Political Theory*. Oxford University Press, pp. 3, 16; Freeden, M. 2003. *Ideology: A Very Short Introduction*. Oxford University Press.

24. Freeden, *Ideologies and Political Theory*, p. 145.

25. Freeden, M. 2017. 'After the Brexit Referendum: Revising Populism as an Ideology'. *Journal of Political Ideologies*, 22(1), pp. 1–11, p. 3.

26. Laclau, *On Populist Reason.*

27. Müller, J.-W. 2017. *What Is Populism?*, Penguin, p. 19.

28. See Laclau, E. 2014. *The Rhetorical Foundations of Society*. Verso.

29. Laclau, *The Rhetorical Foundations of Society*, ch. 6.

30. Calhoun, C., 1982. *The Question of Class Struggle: The Social Foundations of Popular Radicalism*. University of Chicago Press.

31. Mouffe, *For a Left Populism*, p. 3.

32. See Müller, *What Is Populism?*

33. Bobbio, N. 1996. *Left and Right: The Significance of a Political Distinction.* Polity, pp. 2–3.

34. Bobbio, *Left and Right*, p. 10.

35. Bobbio, *Left and Right*, p. 9.

36. Errejón, Í and Mouffe, C. 2016. *Podemos: In the Name of the People.* Lawrence Wishart.

37. 'Alt-right' as a different species than the traditional right, Boris Johnson in the UK and Donald Trump in the US being the poster boys. Where the previous right was economically neoliberal and socially liberal, the alt-right is extreme neoliberal and socially illiberal.

Chapter 2

1. Nunns, A. 2018. *The Candidate*. OR Books, p. 125.

2. Watkins, J. et al. 2017. 'Effects of Health and Social Care Spending Constraints on Mortality in England: A Time Trend Analysis'. *BMJ Open*. Available at: https://bmjopen.bmj.com/content/7/11/e017722.full (accessed 31 January 2020).

3. Nash, K. 2000. *Contemporary Political Sociology*. Blackwell, pp. 102–3.

4. Corbyn, J. 2019. 'We Won the Argument, But I Regret We Didn't Convert That into a Majority for Change'. *The Guardian*. Available at: www.theguardian.com/politics/2019/dec/14/we-won-the-argument-but-i-regret-we-didnt-convert-that-into-a-majority-for-change (accessed 8 December 2020).

5. Laclau, E. 2005. *On Populist Reason*. Verso, p. 10.

6. Gurthie, S. 2014. 'List Ranks the world's Most Miserable Countries'. *The New Daily*. Available at: https://thenewdaily.com.au/news/world/2014/11/10/world-misery-index-2013/#:~:text=Professer%20Hanke%20who%20specialises%20inconflict%20poverty%20or%20starvation%20rates (accessed 29 November 2020).

7. Torcal, M. 2011. 'The Incumbent Electoral Defeat in the 2011 Spanish National Elections: The Effect of the Economic Crisis in an Ideological Polarized Party System'. *Journal of Elections, Public Opinion and Parties*, 24(2), pp. 203–21.

8. Castells, M. 2012. *Networks of Outrage and Hope: Social Movements in the Internet Age*. Polity Press; Gerbaudo, P. 2012. *Tweets and the Streets: Social Media and Contemporary Activism*. Pluto Press; Langman, L. 2013. 'Occupy: A New New Social Movement'. *Current Sociology*, 64(4), pp. 510–24.

9. Lewis, P. and Luce, S. 2012. 'Labor and Occupy Wall Street: An Appraisal of the First Six Months'. *New Labor Forum*, 21(2), pp. 43–9; Mann, K. 2014. 'Social Movement Literature and U.S. Labour: A Reassessment'. *Studies in Social Justice*, 8(2), pp. 165–79. This is not a new argument and Graig Calhoun has discussed the mutual co-existence between nineteenth-century social and labour movements. Calhoun, C. 1993. '"New Social Movements" of the Early Nineteenth Century'. *Social Science History*, 17(3), pp. 385–427.

10. Castells, *Networks of Outrage and Hope*; Gerbaudo, *Tweets and the Streets*.

11. Nash, K. 2000. *Contemporary Political Sociology*. Blackwell.

12. See, e.g., Bosi, L. and Malthamer, S. 2020. 'Political Violence', in Della Porta, D. and Diani, M. (eds) *The Oxford Handbook of Social Movements*, 3rd ed. Blackwell.

13. Melucci, A. 1985. 'The Symbolic Challenges of Contemporary Movements'. *Social Research*, 52, pp. 789–816; Mueller, C. 1994. 'Conflict Networks and the Origins of Women's Liberation', in Larana, E., Johnston, H. and Gusfield, R.J. (eds.) *New Social Movements: From Ideology to Identity*. Temple University Press.

14. Reuters. 2020. 'Timeline: Riots in Britain'. Available at: www.reuters.com/article/us-britain-riots-events/timeline-riots-in-britain-idUSTRE77B1Z420110812 (accessed 29 November 2020).

15. Berman, G. 2014. 'The August 2011 Riots: A Statistical Summary'. Available at: https://commonslibrary.parliament.uk/research-briefings/sn06099/ (accessed 29 November 2020).

16. Home Office. 2011. 'An Overview of Recorded Crimes and Arrests Resulting from Disorder Events in August 2011'.

17. Benyon, J. and Solomos, J. (eds) 1987. *The Roots of Urban Unrest*. Pergamon.

18. Kawalerowicz, J. and Biggs, M. 2015. 'Anarchy in the UK: Economic Deprivation, Social Disorganization, and Political Grievances in the London Riot of 2011'. *Social Forces*, 94(2), pp. 673–98.

19. Kawalerowicz and Briggs, 'Anarchy in the UK'; Neal, C. 2011. 'Bringing Adversity Back in: Economic Breakdown and the Pace of Collective Action'. Annual Meeting at the American Sociological Association, Las Vegas, Nevada.

20. Quoted in Tyler, I. 2013. *Revolting Subjects: Social Abjection and Resistance in Neoliberal britain*. Zed Books, p. 204.

21. Karyotis, G. and Rudig, W. 2018. 'The Three Waves of Anti-austerity Protest in Greece, 2010–2015'. *Political Studies*, 16(2), pp. 158–69.

22. The quotes in this part are from 25 interviews with Greek activists who participated both in the December 2008 riots and in the Indignados movement in 2011. The names have been changed.

23. The timing of the interviews may be significant because when we look back at our lives we all try to connect everything in a coherent narrative.

24. Lyrintzis, C. 2011. 'Greek Politics in the Era of Economic Crisis: Reassessing Causes and Effects'. Hellenic Observatory, GreeSE Paper No 45; Karamichas, J. 2009. 'The December Riots in Greece'. *Social Movement Studies*, 8(3): 289–93.

25. Lacan, J. 2016. *Anxiety*. Polity Press; Bert, O. 2017. 'Protests, "Acting-Out", Group Psychology, Surplus Enjoyment and Neoliberal Capitalism'. *PINS (Psychology and Society)*, 53, pp. 30–50.

26. See Laclau, E. and Mouffe, C. 1985. *Hegemony and Socialist Strategy*. Verso, pp. 129–31.

27. Calhoun, C. 2013. 'Occupy Wall Street in Perspective'. *British Journal of Sociology*, 64(1), pp. 26–38.

28. Occupy London, Initial Statement. Available at: https://occupylondon. org.uk/about/statements/initial-statement/ (accessed 16 August 2019).

29. Occupy London, United for Global Democracy. Available at: https:// occupylondon.org.uk/about/statements/global-democracy-statement/ (accessed 16 August 2019).

30. Frazer, G. 2011. 'Occupy St Paul's: No Church Should Insulate Itself from Raw Human Need'. *The Guardian*. Available at: www.theguardian. com/commentisfree/belief/2011/nov/17/st-pauls-occupy-movement-christianity (accessed 16 August 2019).

31. Gutierrez, G. 1974. *A Theology of Liberation*. SCM Press.

32. See Gitlin, T. 2013. 'Occupy's Predicament: The Moment and the Prospects for the Movement'. *The British Journal of Sociology*, 64(1), pp. 3–25; Calhoun, 'Occupy Wall Street', 2013.

33. Calhoun, 'Occupy Wall Street', 2013.

34. Gitlin, 'Occupy's Predicament', p. 3.
35. Gitlin, 'Occupy's Predicament', p. 3.
36. Prentoulis, M. and Thomassen, L. 2014. 'Autonomy and Hegemony in the Squares: The 2011 Protests in Greece and Spain', in Kioupkiolis, A. and Katsambekis, G. (eds) *Radical Democracy and Collective Movements Today: The Biopolitics of the Multitude versus the Hegemony of the People*. Ashgate, pp. 213–34.
37. Papariga, A. 2011. 'The Need for Political Struggle'. *Rizospastis*, 31 May; Anonymous. 2011. 'For the Movement of the Squares'. *Rizospastis*, 29 May.
38. Communist Party of Greece. Available at: www.kke.gr/eklogika_apotelesmata/apotelesmata_ethnikon_eklogon?act=4&tab=1 (accessed 19 April 2019).
39. The site had a number of functions: it gave visibility to the movement, published the decisions of the assemblies thus enabling organization and transparency, connected the periphery squares (in smaller towns and cities) with the central sites of Syntagma-Athens and Sol-Madrid and it was an essential tool for activists.
40. Errejón, I. and Mouffe, C. 2016. *Podemos: In the Name of the People*. Lawrence Wishart, pp. 70–1.
41. Theodossopoulos, D. 2014. 'The Poetics of Indignation in Greece: Anti-austerity Protest and Accountability', in N. Werner, K. Spellman-Poots and M. Webb (eds) *The Political Aesthetics of Global Protest: The Arab Spring and Beyond*. Edinburgh University Press, p. 370.
42. Kyriakidou, M. and Olivas Osuna, J. J. 2014. 'Press Coverage and Civic Engagement During the Euro Crisis: The Case of the Indignados'. *International Journal of Media & Cultural Politics*, 10(2), pp. 213–20, p. 215.
43. Theodossopoulos, 'Poetics of Indignation', pp. 370–1.
44. Karyotis, G. and Rudig, W. 2018. 'The Three Waves of Anti-austerity Protest in Greece, 2010–2015'. *Political Studies*, 16(2), pp. 158–69.
45. Public Issue. 2011. *Το Κίνημα των Αγανακτισμένων Πολιτών: Έρευνα κοινής γνώμης για τις νέες μορφές της κοινωνικής κινητοποίησης* [The Movement of the Indignant Citizens: Public Opinion Survey on New Forms of Social Mobilisation]. *Flash Barometer*, 159, pp. 7–10. Available at: www.skai.gr/files/1/PDF/aganaktismenoi.pdf (accessed 15 October 2015), quoted in Karyotis and Rudig, 'Three Waves'.
46. Negri, T. 2011. Reflexiones acerca del 15M, 4 June. Available at: http://old.kaosenlared.net/noticia/reflexiones-acerca-del-15m (accessed 3 February 2012); Hardt, M. and Negri, A. 2011. 'The Fight for "Real Democracy" at the Heart of Occupy Wall Street'. *Foreign Affairs*, 11 October. Available at: www.foreignaffairs.com/articles/136399/michael-hardt-andantonio-negri/the-fight-for-real-democracy-at-the-heart-of-occupy-wall-street?page=show (accessed 25 March 2012).

47. Prentoulis, M. and Thomassen, L. 2014. 'Autonomy and Hegemony in the Squares: The 2011 Protests in Greece and Spain', in Kioupkiolis, A. and Katsambekis, G. (eds) *Radical Democracy and Collective Movements Today*. Ashgate, pp. 213–34; Prentoulis, M. and Thomassen, L. 2013. 'Political Theory in the Square: Protest, Representation and Subjectification'. *Contemporary Political Theory*, 12(3), pp. 166–84.
48. Alexis Tsipras, 11 July 2015.
49. Massey, D. 2015. 'Vocabularies of the Economy', in Hall, S., Massey, D. and Rustin, M. (eds) *After Neoliberalism? The Kilburn Manifesto*. Lawrence Wishart.
50. Katz, R.S. and Mair, P. 1994. *How Parties Organize*. Sage, pp. 7–8.
51. Crouch, C. 2010. *Post-democracy*. Polity Press.

Chapter 3

1. There is a lot of political disagreement in the public discourse in Greece around this point. The reason is that right-wing governments often try to promote the 'horseshow theory', namely that far left and far right are the same. In recent times this has also been used as a way for the Greek right-wing government to disassociate itself from the Nazi party Golden Dawn on the one hand, and attack Syriza on the other. In this narrative both Syriza and Golden Dawn are responsible for the indignant movement. This theory has been rejected by the left and rightly so, arguing that Golden Dawn was against the movement. However, we have to accept that the diversity of the indignant movement (and other movements for that matter) and the fact that movements are not insulated does not prohibit very different ideological universes from meeting in public demonstrations. When the identity of the movement is crystalized, those with no interest in democratic change drop out.
2. Ranciere, J. 1999. *Disagreement: Politics and Philosophy*. University of Minesota Press, p. 40.
3. Prentoulis, M. and Thomassen, L. 2013. 'Political Theory in the Square: Protest, Representation and Subjectification'. *Contemporary Political Theory*, 12(3), pp. 166–84.
4. Prentoulis and Thomassen, 'Political Theory in the Square'.
5. Errejón, I. and Mouffe, C. 2016. *Podemos: In the Name of the People*. Lawrence Wishart, pp. 72–3.
6. See Calhoun, C. 1993. '"New Social Movements" of the Early Nineteenth Century'. *Social Science History*, 17(3), pp. 385–427.
7. Kitschelt, H. 1990. 'New Social Movements and "New Politics" Parties in Western Europe', in Dalton, R.J. and Kuechler, M. (eds) *Challenging the Political Order: New Social and Political Movements in Western Democracies*. Polity, pp. 179–208.
8. Kitschelt, 'New Social Movements', p. 202.

9. Independent Greeks, a nationalist, right-wing party formed in 2012 by Panos Kamenos, former MP of the right-wing New Democracy. As a new party ANEL had not been implicated in the build-up to the Greek crisis.

10. Avgi Newsroom. 2019. 'iSYRIZA: Καλώς ορίσατε στη νέα εποχή'. Available at: https://www.avgi.gr/arheio/335158_isyriza-kalos-orisate-sti-nea-epohi.

11. I have written elsewhere about the need for a grassroots approach. See, e.g., Prentoulis, M. 2015. 'Get Back to Grassroots, Syriza – and Show Us a Radical Vision to Transform Greece'. *The Guardian*, 23 September. Available at: www.theguardian.com/commentisfree/2015/sep/23/syriza-election-back-grassroots-transform-greece-tsipras (accessed 22 February 2020).

12. Kioupkiolis, A. 2019. 'Late Modern Adventures of Leftish Populism in Spain: The Case of Podemos, 2014–2018', in Katsambekis, G. and Kioupkiolis, A. (eds) *The Populist Radical Left in Europe*. Routledge, pp. 47–72.

13. Galdon Clavell, G. 2015. Podemos y la politica de la technologia. *Revista Teknokultura*, 12(1), pp. 111–19.

14. Della Porta, D. et al. 2017. *Movement Parties Against Austerity*. Polity, p. 23.

15. See Podemos. 2020. *Organización – Podemos*. Available at: https://podemos.info/conoce/?lang=en (accessed 10 December 2020).

16. Kioupkiolis, 'Late Modern Adventures', p. 63.

17. The equivalent of the general conference of the 'older' type of parties which was held between October and November of the same year.

18. See Publico. 2014. 'Podemos ya es la tercera fuerza en afiliados con 100.000 registrados'. Available at: www.publico.es/politica/ya-tercera-fuerza-afiliados-100.html (accessed 17 September 2019).

19. A *marea* is a tide, a protest (occupations, strikes, etc.) organized by activist on a particular issue. In the wake of 15M, a number of *mareas* were organized against the Spanish government, for example the *marea blanca* (white tide) against cuts to the budget of the country. Internally they are organized by assemblies.

20. En Comú (in common) are electoral coalitions and citizens platforms at municipal level.

21. He had been the general coordinator of United Left, later close to the 15M movement before joining Podemos. He resigned from Podemos in 2015.

22. Part of the Anticapitalistas organization in Podemos and Podemos' Andalusian candidate in the 2015 and 2018 parliamentary elections.

23. One of the five Podemos MEPs elected in 2014. In the 2019 national election he was elected to the Congress of Deputies.

24. Cabanillas, A. 2016. 'Vistalegre I vs. Vistalegre II: diez diferecias dos anos despues'. *El Independiente*. Available at: www.elindependiente.com/

politica/2016/12/10/vistalegre-i-vs-vistalegre-ii-10-diferencias-dos-
anos-despues/ (accessed 10 December 2020).

25. See, e.g. Cannon, B. 2009. *Hugo Chavez and the Bolivarian Revolution*. Manchester University Press.

26. Franze, J. 2019. 'Adios, Vistalegre I'. ctxt, 206. Available at: https://ctxt. es/es/20190130/Firmas/24174/podemos-vistalegre-I-voluntad-politica-javier-franze.htm (accessed 10 September 2019).

27. García Agustín, Ó. and Briziarelli, M. 2019. 'Introduction: Wind of Change: Podemos, Its Dreams and Its Politics', in García Agustín, Ó. and Briziarelli, M. (eds) *Podemos and the New Political Cycle: Left-Wing Populism and Anti-establishment Politics*. Palgrave Macmillan, p. 12.

28. Íñigo Errejón finally split from Podemos in September 2019 and launched a new party, Más País, roughly translated as 'More Country', aiming to assist PSOE and his leader Pedro Sanchez in forming a government after the 10 November 2019 general election.

29. Unidas Podemos (feminine) before the November 2019 general election.

30. Cabanillas, 'Vistalegre I vs. Vistalegre II'.

31. Manin, B. 1997. *The Principles of Representative Democracy*. Cambridge University Press.

32. Kioupkiolis, 'Late Modern Adventures', p. 64.

33. Errejón, and Mouffe, *Podemos*, p. 73.

34. Cabanillas, 'Vistalegre I vs. Vistalegre II'.

35. Franze, J. 2019. 'Adio's Vistalegre I'. *Contexto y Accio'n*. Available at: https://ctxt.es/es/20190130/Firmas/24174/podemos-vistalegre-I-voluntad-politica-javier-franze.htm (accessed 13 December 2020).

36. Cabanillas, 'Vistalegre I vs. Vistalegre II'.

37. Balabanidis, G. 2015. *Eurocommunism*. Polis, pp. 131–5.

38. United Democratic Left, a coalition of communist and non-communist left founded 1951–89. The biggest legal left party before the dictatorship (1967–74) which never regained its support after 1974.

39. Milios, J. 2016. 'Does Social Democracy Hold Up Half the Sky? The Decline of PASOK and the Rise of SYRIZA in Greece', in Schmidt, I. (ed.) *The Three Worlds of Social Democracy: A Global View*. Pluto Press, pp. 127–45.

40. Tsakatika, M. and Eleftheriou, C. 2013. 'The Radical Left's Turn towards Civil Society in Greece: One Strategy, Two Paths'. *South European Society and Politics*, 18(1), pp. 81–99.

41. Syriza. 2013. *10* (Ιδρυτικό) Συνέδριο. ΠΟΛΙΤΙΚΗ ΑΠΟΦΑΣΗ. Available at: www.syriza.gr/pdfs/politiki_apofasi_idrytikou_synedriou_syriza.pdf (acccessed 22 January 2021).

42. Wainwright, H. 2018. *A New Politics from the Left*. Polity Press.

43. Momentum. 2020. 'About – Momentum'. Available at: https://peoplesmomentum.com/about/ (accessed 14 December 2020).

44. Garland, J. 2017. 'Labour's New Model Party', in Perryman, M. (ed.) *The Corbyn Effect*. Lawrence Wishart, p. 70.

45. Kentish, B. 2018. 'Jeremy Corbyn Backs Momentum Calls for "Changes" that Could Make it Easier to Deselect Labour MPs'. *Independent*. Available at: www.independent.co.uk/news/uk/politics/jeremy-corbyn-labour-mp-deselection-momentum-nec-vote-conference-a8521141.html (accessed 14 December 2020).

46. Pettitt, R. 2017. 'Losing Momentum? The Power Struggles that Are Hobbling the Corbyn Movement'. *Democratic Audit*. Available at: www.democraticaudit.com/2017/03/07/losing-momentum-the-power-struggles-that-are-hobbling-the-corbyn-movement/ (accessed 14 December 2020).

47. Watts, J. and Bale, T. 2019. 'Populism as an Intra-party Phenomenon: The British Labour Party under Jeremy Corbyn'. *The British Journal of Politics and International Relations*, 21(1), pp. 99–115.

Chapter 4

1. Laclau, E. and Mouffe, C., 1985. *Hegemony and Socialist Strategy*. Verso; Mouffe, C. 1999. 'Deliberative Democracy or Agonistic Pluralism?', *Social Research*, 66(3), pp. 745–58.

2. See Hall, S., Massey, D. and Rustin, M. 2015. *After Neoliberalism? The Kilburn Manifesto*. Lawrence Wishart.

3. Schmidt, I. 2016. 'Introduction: Social Democracy and Uneven Development – Theoretical Reflections on the Three Worlds of Social Democracy', in Schmidt, I. (ed.) *The Three Worlds of Social Democracy: A Global View*. Pluto, p. 17.

4. See Tsakalotos, E. 1998. 'The Political Economy of Social Democratic Economic Policies: The PASOK Experiment in Greece'. *Oxford Review of Economic Policy*, 14(1), pp. 114–37; Milios, J. 2016. 'Does Social Democracy Hold Up Half the Sky? The Decline of PASOK and the rise of SYRIZA in Greece', in Schmidt, I. (ed.) *The Three Worlds of Social Democracy: A Global View*. Pluto, pp. 127–45.

5. Lyrintzis, C. 1987. 'The Power of Populism'. *European Journal of Political Research*, 15, pp. 667–86, p. 668.

6. Admittedly, since citizenship in Greece (as in Germany) is defined by 'genus' this law did not help the Bulgarians or ethnic Macedonians – a debate that was destined to return when the Syriza government signed a treaty with North Macedonia in 2019, infuriating the nationalist right (and part of the nationalist left) who used it as a weapon against Syriza.

7. In her conversation with Errejón on the issue of national populism in *Podemos: In the Name of the People* (2016), about the differences between European and South American societies, Mouffe argues that the latter have excluded big parts of the population from democratic processes (p. 80), but the same can be said for societies like Greece haunted by the spectre of successive dictatorships.

8. ΠΑΣΟΚ. 1974. *Ιδρυτική Διακήρυξη | ΠΑΣΟΚ*. Available at: http://pasok. gr/diakhryxh/ (accessed 14 December 2020).
9. Tsakalotos, 'Political Economy', p. 116.
10. Milios, J. 2016, Does social Democracy Hold Up Half the Sky?, p. 131.
11. Tsakalotos, 'Political Economy'.
12. ΠΑΣΟΚ, *Ιδρυτική Διακήρυξη*.
13. Milios, 'Does Social Democracy Hold Up Half the Sky?'
14. See Torcal, M. 2014. 'The Incumbent Electoral Defeat in the 2011 Spanish National Elections: The Effect of the Economic Crisis in an Ideological Polarized Party System'. *Journal of Elections, Public Opinion & Parties*, 24(2), pp. 203–21, p. 204.
15. Rendueles, C. and Sola, J. 2018. 'The Rise of Podemos: Promises, Constraints, and Dilemmas', in García Agustín, Ó. and Briziarelli, M. (eds) *Podemos and the New Political Cycle: Left-Wing Populism and Anti-establishment Politics*. Palgrave-Macmillan, pp. 27–8.
16. The Spanish dictator Franco died in 1975, and in 1978 the Spanish constitution was approved. PSOE came to power in 1982. The Greek dictatorship ended in 1974 and PASOK came to power in 1981.
17. PSOE in 1976 had as its slogan 'mass, Marxist and democratic'. When in the 1979 Congress Gonzales tried to abandon Marxism he found a lot of resistance. He momentarily resigned but after some organizational reforms the party voted in favour of the abandonment of Marxism and Gonzales resumed as leader. See Share, D. 1988. 'Dilemmas of Social Democracy in the 1980s: The Spanish Socialist Workers Party in Comparative Perspective'. *Comparative Political Studies*, 21, pp. 408–35; Sanchez-Cuenca, I. 2004. 'Party Moderation and Politicians' Ideological Rigidity'. *Party Politics*, 10(3), pp. 325–42.
18. Rendueles and Sola, 'Rise of Podemos', pp. 30–1.
19. See Mato, J.F. 2011. 'Spain: Fragmented Unemployment Protection in a Segmented Labour Market', in Clasen, J. and Clegg, D. (eds) *Regulating the Risk of Unemployment: National Adaptations to Post-industrial Labour Markets in Europe*. Oxford University Press, pp. 164–86.
20. Marx, P. and Schumacher, G. 2013. 'Will to Power? Intra-party Conflict in Social Democratic Parties and the Choice for Neoliberal Policies in Germany, the Netherlands and Spain (1980–2010)'. *European Political Science Review*, 5(1), pp. 151–73.
21. Burger, S. 2014. 'Former Caja Madrid Directors Accused of Misusing Company Credit Card'. *The Guardian*. Available at: www.theguardian. com/business/2014/oct/09/former-caja-directors-accused-credit-card-misuse-bankia (accessed 15 December 2020).
22. There is an extensive academic literature that tries to draws these distinctions based on rational choice theory, with underlying premises that are very different from those of populist theory, around debates over issues such as how rational the political choices we make are and what they are motivated by. Downs, A. 1957. *An Economic Theory of Democracy*.

Harper and Row (vote-seeking parties); Wittman, D.A. 1973. 'Parties as Utility Maximizers'. *American Political Science Review*, 67, pp. 490–8; Wittman, D.A. 1983. 'Candidate Motivation: A Synthesis of Alternative Theories'. *American Political Science Review*, 77, pp. 142–57 (policy-seeking parties). Another category is office-seeking parties, related to government coalition theories like Riker, W.H. 1962. *The Theory of Political Coalitions*. Yale University Press.

23. Guilbert, J. 2019. 'The Only Way for Labour to Win Is by "Ditching" Labourism'. *The Guardian*. Available at: www.theguardian.com/comment isfree/2019/dec/31/only-way-labour-win-ditch-labourism-corbyn (accessed 15 December 2020).

24. We can find this tendency to use the term 'populism', apart from in the media and academic literature I mentioned earlier, in many contemporary writings. See, e.g., Perryman, M. 2017. 'The Great Moving Left Show', in Perryman, M. (ed.) *The Corbyn Effect*. Lawrence Wishart, p. 16. Also see Stubbs, D. 2016. *1996 and the End of History*. Repeater Books.

25. Bulman, M. 2016. 'Labour Plans to Relaunch Jeremy Corbyn as Left-Wing Populist in Bid to Seize on Anti-establishment Sentiment'. *Independent*. Available at: www.independent.co.uk/news/uk/politics/labour-jeremy-corbyn-jon-trickett-left-wing-populist-anti-establish ment-general-election-a7478516.html (accessed 15 December 2020).

26. See Melanchon's speech. Available at: https://2018.theworldtransformed. org/sessions/conversation-with-jean-luc-melenchon (accessed 8 January 2020).

27. Manuela Carmena, a left-wing former judge. She headed the Ahora Madrid citizens' platform at the local elections of 2015 and she was the Mayor of Madrid from 2015 to 2019.

28. See Gil, A. 2016. 'Unidos Podemos fracasa en el sorpasso a un PSOE que logra el peor resultado histórico en escaños'. *El diario*. Available at: www.eldiario.es/politica/unidos-podemos-sorpasso-psoe-historia_1_ 3926830.html (accessed 15 December 2020).

29. Torcal, M. 2014. 'The Incumbent Electoral Defeat in the 2011 Spanish National Elections: The Effect of the Economic Crisis in an Ideological Polarized Party System'. *Journal of Elections, Public Opinion & Parties*, 24(2), pp. 203–21.

30. Dean, J.M. and Maiguashca, B. 2017. 'Corbyn's Labour and the Populism Question'. *Renewal: A Journal of Social Democracy*, 25(3/4), pp. 56–65.

31. Dorey, P. 2017. 'Jeremy Corbyn Confounds His Critics: Explaining the Labour Party's Remarkable Resurgence in the 2017 Election'. *British Politics*, 12, pp. 308–34.

32. Casero-Ripollés, A., Feenstra, R.A. and Tormey, S. 2016. 'Old and New Media Logics in an Electoral Campaign: The Case of Podemos and the Two-Way Street Mediatization of Politics'. *The International Journal of Press/Politics*, 21(3), pp. 378–97.

33. What the *circulos* voted for at the Vistalegre I citizens' assembly resulted in the adoption of resolutions by the party, which were the five most voted, all of which were submitted by circles. Every member could vote for five resolutions. The approved resolutions were on improving public education (45 per cent), on anti-corruption measures (42 per cent), on the right to housing (38 per cent), on improving public healthcare (31 per cent) and on auditing and restructuring the debt (23 per cent).

34. This cleavage is also present in Greece but in a different context: there is not the level of autonomy that different regions in Spain have and politics outside two or three major Greek cities like Thessaloniki are following the lead of the centre. At the local level, local 'influencers' (in the sense of patronage, nepotism, etc.) are voted for by locals in return for favours which are lent to one party or the other.

35. Rodríguez-Teruel, J. Barrio, A. and Barberà, O. 2016. 'Fast and Furious: Podemos' Quest for Power in Multi-level Spain'. *South European Society and Politics*, 21(4), pp. 561–85.

36. See Sampedro, V. 2015. 'Podemos, de la invisibilidad a la sobre-exposición' [Podemos, from Invisibility to Overexposure]. *Teknokultura*, 12(1), pp. 137–45.

37. Pablo Iglesias' TV talk show, which was first transmitted by two community TV channels, Tele K and Canal 33, then streamed online and finally disseminated via YouTube. In the end it got Podemos the attention of mainstream media and Pablo Iglesias became a well-known figure on national TV.

38. Kioupkiolos, A. and Katsambekis, G. 2018. 'Radical Left Populism from the Margins to the Mainstream: A Comparison of Syriza and Podemos', in García Agustín and Briziarelli (eds) *Podemos and the New Political Cycle*, pp. 201–26.

39. Synaspismos. 2012. 'Εκλογικο Προγραμμα Συριζα Ενωτικο Κοινωνικο Μετωπο – Εκλογέσ 6ης Μαΐου 2012'. Available at: www.syn.gr/gr/keimeno.php?id=26945 (accessed 10 December 2020).

40. Synaspismos, 'Εκλογικο0'.

41. Synaspismos, 'Εκλογικο'.

42. Synaspismos, 'Εκλογικο'.

43. Synaspismos, 'Εκλογικο'.

44. Tsipras, A. 2015. 'Central Electoral Campaign Speech, Omonoia Square, Athens 22/01/15'. Available at: www.youtube.com/watch?v=UohhwR7MmlY (accessed 12 December 2019).

45. Boukala, S. and Dimitra Dimitrakopoulou, D. 2017. 'The Politics of Fear vs. the Politics of Hope: Analysing the 2015 Greek Election and Referendum Campaigns'. *Critical Discourse Studies*, 14(1), pp. 39–55.

46. Tsipras, 'Central Electoral Campaign Speech'.

47. Tsipras, 'Central Electoral Campaign Speech'.

48. Moffitt, B. and Tormey, S. 2014. 'Rethinking Populism: Politics, Mediatisation and Political Style'. *Political Studies*, 62(2), pp. 381–97.

49. Dean and Maiguashca, 'Corbyn's Labour'.
50. Walker, A. 2019. 'All Hail Stormzy for Historic Glastonbury Performance'. *The Guardian*. Available at: https://www.theguardian.com/music/2019/jun/29/stormzy-historic-glastonbury-performance (accessed 15 December 2020).
51. Dorey, 'Jeremy Corbyn Confounds His Critics'.
52. Crines, A. 2015. 'Jeremy Corbyn's Rhetoric Is Effective Because His Style of Engagement Contrasts So Markedly with the Other Candidates'. LSE. Available at: https://blogs.lse.ac.uk/politicsandpolicy/jeremy-corbyns-rhetoric-is-effective-because-his-style-of-engagement-contrasts-so-markedly-with-the-other-candidates/ (accessed 21 March 20).
53. Editorial. 2016. 'The Guardian View on Traingate: Jeremy Corbyn's Search for Standing'. *The Guardian*. Available at: www.theguardian.com/commentisfree/2016/aug/24/the-guardian-view-on-traingate-jeremy-corbyns-search-for-standing (accessed 15 December 2020); Stewart, H. and Syal, R. 2016. 'Virgin Trains Controversy "Has Helped Jeremy Corbyn's Leadership Bid"'. *The Guardian*. Available at: www.theguardian.com/politics/2016/aug/24/virgin-rail-controversy-has-helped-jeremy-corbyns-leadership-bid (accessed 15 December 2020).
54. See Gill, M. 2016. 'Jeremy Corbyn Unreachable During Traingate Because He Was "Making Jam"'. *Huffington Post*. Available at: www.huffingtonpost.co.uk/entry/corbyn-unreachable-during-traingate-because-he-was-making-jam_uk_57beaaa3e4b0ba22a4d34708 (accessed 15 December 2020).
55. Chorley, M. 2019. 'Jeremy Corbyn's Gone from Making Jam to Creating a Pickle'. *The Times*. Available at: www.thetimes.co.uk/article/jeremy-corbyns-gone-from-making-jam-to-creating-a-pickle-pff3bf8kb (accessed 15 December 2020).
56. Cammaerts, B. 2016. 'Journalistic Representation of Jeremy Corbyn in the British Press'. LSE. Available at: www.lse.ac.uk/media-and-communications/research/research-projects/representations-of-jeremy-corbyn (accessed 21 March 2020).
57. Skinner, G. and Gottfried, G. 2020. 'Jeremy Corbyn's Leader Image Ratings Improve since Last Conference Season, Theresa May's Get Worse'. Ipsos MORI. Available at: www.ipsos.com/ipsos-mori/en-uk/jeremy-corbyns-leader-image-ratings-improve-last-conference-season-theresa-mays-get-worse (accessed 15 December 2020).
58. Tolhurst, A. 2020. 'Jeremy Corbyn "Most Unpopular Opposition Leader of Past 45 Years", Says Poll'. *Politics Home*. Available at: www.politicshome.com/news/article/jeremy-corbyn-most-unpopular-opposition-leader-of-past-45-years-says-poll (accessed 15 December 2020); Sabbagh, D. 2019. 'Johnson and Corbyn Locked in Unpopularity Contest, Polls Suggest'. *The Guardian*. Available at: www.theguardian.

com/politics/2019/nov/19/boris-johnson-jeremy-corbyn-unpopularity-contest-polls (accessed 15 December 2020).

59. Rodgers, S. 2018. 'Why Won't Jeremy Corbyn Just Adopt the Full IHRA Definition?' *LabourList*. Available at: https://labourlist.org/2018/07/why-wont-jeremy-corbyn-just-adopt-the-full-ihra-definition/ (accessed 15 December 2020).

Chapter 5

1. For an accessible discussion on populist theory see Tormey, S. 2019. *Populism*. Oneworld.
2. For the particularities of Eurocommunist parties see Belantis, D. 2014. 'The Left and Power: the "Democratic Road" to Socialism'. *Topos*, pp. 218–24.
3. See Owen, R. 1841. *Outline of the Rational System of Society*. A. Heywood.
4. It is worth mentioning here that Alexis Tsipras and Syriza, although members of the European Left party, do have the status of 'observer' in the Party of European Socialists. Syriza had a lot of support from the European Socialists despite the hostility of PASOK towards them. It also signposts the attempt (1) to create an alliance of progressive forces in Greece led by Syriza (which the Greek socialists have refused) and (2) of Syriza to occupy the political space that PASOK lost. Michalopoulos, S. 2017. 'PES President: Unlike EPP, Socialists Do Not Impose Decisions on Member Parties'. Euractiv.com. Available at: www.euractiv.com/section/future-eu/news/pes-president-unlike-epp-socialists-do-not-impose-decisions-on-member-parties/ (accessed 15 December 2020).
5. Beatrice (1858–1943) and Sidney Webb (1859–1947), socialists and labour historians, founders of the London School of Economics and the Fabian society.
6. LabourList. 2014. '10 Of The Best Tony Benn Quotes'. Available at: https://labourlist.org/2014/03/10-of-the-best-tony-benn-quotes/ (accessed 15 December 2020).
7. Sakellaropoulos, S. 2001. *Greece after the Dictatorship*. Livanis.
8. Belantis, 'The Left and Power', pp. 130–1.
9. Belantis, 'The Left and Power', p. 133.
10. Labour Party. 2017. *For the Many Not the Few*. Available at: https://labour.org.uk/wp-content/uploads/2017/10/labour-manifesto-2017.pdf (accessed 15 December 2020), p. 16.
11. Tsakalotos, E. 1998. 'The Political Economy of Social Democratic Economic Policies: The PASOK Experiment in Greece'. *Oxford Review of Economic Policy*, 14(1), pp. 114–37, p. 116.
12. Belantis, 'The Left and Power', pp. 133–4.
13. Labour Party, *For the Many Not the Few*.
14. Labour Party, *For the Many Not the Few*, p. 19.

15. Cole, G.D.H. 1955. *Socialist Thought: The Forerunners 1789–1850*. Macmillan & Co. Ltd, pp. 120–1.
16. Prentoulis, M. and Kyriakidou, M. 2019. 'Media and Collective Action in Greece: From Indignation to Solidarity'. *International Journal of Communication*, 13, pp. 1–19.
17. For some very interesting interviews with those involved in such experiments see the documentary *Another World is Possible*. 2013. Iliosporoi. Available at: www.youtube.com/watch?v=fX8cEfV8l4U (accessed 10 March 20).
18. Whyatt, T. 2019. 'Foodbank App Run by Newly Elected Tory MP Charges Charities to Use It'. *Independent*. Available at: www.independent.co.uk/news/uk/politics/foodbank-app-miriam-cates-mp-conservative-general-election-universal-credit-a9245901.html (accessed 15 December 2020).
19. Putnam, R.D. 1993. *Making Democracy Work: Civil Traditions in Modern Italy*. Princeton University Press.
20. Mouzelis, N. 1978. *Modern Greece: Facets of Underdevelopment*. Macmillan.
21. Tsakalotos, 'Political Economy'.
22. www.solidarity4all.gr.
23. I refer to the R. Antonopoulou Bill of 2016 – N.4430/16 – aiming at the development of the social and solidarity economy sector, through the creation of a favourable environment, which would facilitate the participation of those citizens who wish to engage in productive activities. These activities would show respect to both human beings and the environment and be organised through the dissemination of democracy, equality, solidarity and cooperation between participants and local communities. Opengov.gr. 2016. 'Σχέδιο Νόμου "Κοινωνική Και Αλληλέγγυα Οικονομία Και Ανάπτυξη Των Φορέων Της" | Εργασίας Και Κοινωνικών Υποθέσεων'. Available at: www.opengov.gr/minlab/?p=3381 (accessed 15 December 2020).
24. Τσακαλώτος, Ε. 2019. 'Η ευρωπαϊκή αριστερά πρέπει να συζητήσει εναλλακτικά μοντέλα παραγωγής'. *Εφ.Συν*. Available at: http://«Η ευρωπαϊκή αριστερά πρέπει να συζητήσει εναλλακτικά μοντέλα παραγωγής» (accessed 15 December 2020).
25. TVXS – TV Χωρίς Σύνορα. 2020. 'Κοινωνικό Ιατρείο Ελληνικού: Επιστρέφουμε Στην Κυβέρνηση Το Τελεσίγραφο'. Available at: https://tvxs.gr/news/ellada/koinoniko-iatreio-ellinikoy-epistrefoyme-stin-kybernisi-telesigrafo-kai-dinoyme-tin-diki (accessed 15 December 2020).
26. Αυγή. 2015. 'Το "παράλληλο πρόγραμμα" του ΣΥΡΙΖΑ'. Available at: www.avgi.gr/politiki/154641_parallilo-programma-toy-syriza (accessed 15 December 2020).
27. Αυγή, 'Το "παράλληλο πρόγραμμα" του ΣΥΡΙΖΑ'.
28. Press Office. 2017. 'Two Years of a Left Government'. 24 January.

29. Before the crisis pensioners and employees were receiving a 'thirteenth' wage, a Christmas bonus if you will, which was cut during the crisis.

30. Press Office, 'Two Years'.

31. Naftemporiki. 2019. 'Privatizations in Greece: Some Moving Forward, Others Struggling'. Available at: www.naftemporiki.gr/story/1533221/ privatizations-in-greece-some-moving-forward-others-struggling (accessed 15 December 2020).

32. Kadritzke, N. 2016. 'The Deception of Privatisations in Greece'. *Green European Journal*. Available at: www.greeneuropeanjournal.eu/the-deception-of-privatisation-in-greece/ (accessed 15 July 20).

33. Aljazeera.com. 2020. 'Spain Introduces Basic Income Scheme to Tackle Poverty'. Available at: www.aljazeera.com/economy/2020/5/30/ spain-introduces-basic-income-scheme-to-tackle-poverty (accessed 15 December 2020); Casla, K. 2020. 'Spain's New Minimum Income Scheme: A Victory and a Historic Failure'. *Open Democracy*. Available at: www. opendemocracy.net/en/can-europe-make-it/spains-new-minimum-income-scheme-a-victory-and-a-historic-failure/ (accessed 15 December 2020).

34. Specialised surgeries operate as the first contact for patients at public hospitals rather than the GP surgeries that we have in Britain.

35. Press Office. 2015. 'Κυριες Πτυχες Κυβερνητικου Εργου Το Πρωτο Πενταμηνο'. Press release.

36. Chrysopoulos, P. 2020. 'Novartis Case Closes in US with Deal Excluding Greek Bribe Allegations'. *Greek Reporter*. Available at: https://greece. greekreporter.com/2020/06/26/novartis-case-closes-in-us-with-deal-excluding-greek-bribe-allegations/ (accessed 15 December 2020).

37. Keep Talking Greece. 2020. 'Greece Prosecutes the Prosecutor Investigating Novartis Bribery Scandal'. *Keep Talking Greece*. Available at: www.keeptalkinggreece.com/2020/07/16/greece-prosecutes-prosecutor-novartis-scandal/ (accessed 15 December 2020).

38. Hallin, D.C. and Mancini, P. 2004. *Comparing Media Systems: Three Models of Media and Politics*. Cambridge University Press.

39. Press Office. 2017. 'In Relation to Mass Media and Kyriakos Mitsotakis'. 20 January.

40. Minister Nikos Pappas and Deputy Minister Lefteris Kretsos.

41. Αυγή. 2018. 'Λ. Κρέτσος: Επιβεβαίωση της νομιμότητας, συνταγματικότητας και της ορθότητας της αδειοδότησης των καναλιών από το ΣτΕ'. Available at: www.avgi.gr/arheio/296266_l-kretsos-epibebaiosi-tis-nomimotitas-syntagmatikotitas-kai-tis-orthotitas-tis (accessed 15 December 2020); Νταρζανου, Α. 2018. 'Κανάλια 'δεν πληρώνω' και πάλι'. *Αυγη*. Available at: www.avgi.gr/article/10838/ 9449998/kanalia-den-plerono-kai-pali (accessed 15 December 2020).

42. The case was discussed by two of my interviewees (journalists associated with Syriza) who were infuriated by the whole story and considered it

typical of the 'war' declared against Syriza by the vested interests of the country.

43. Foucault, M. 2008. *The Birth of Biopolitics: Lectures at the Collège de France, 1978–9.* Palgrave.

44. Eklundh, E. 2018. 'Populism, Hegemony, and the Phantasmatic Sovereign: The Ties between Nationalism and Left-Wing Populism', in García Agustín, Ó. and Briziarelli, M. (eds) *Podemos and the New Political Cycle: Left-Wing Populism and Anti-establishment Politics.* Palgrave Macmillan, p. 125.

45. Reuters. 2015. 'Podemos-Backed Madrid Mayor Halts Social Housing Evictions'. Available at: www.reuters.com/article/us-spain-evictions-idUSKCN0Q21WZ20150728 (accessed 15 December 2020).

46. The original Katseli Bill (N.3869/2010) ended in 2014. It was revised and activated again between 2016 and 2018 by the Stathakis Bill.

47. Thompson, M. 2020. 'What's So New about New Municipalism?' *Progress in Human Geography,* forthcoming.

48. Forman, E., Gran, E. and Outryve, S. 2020. 'Socialism in More than One City'. *Dissent,* 67(1), pp. 134–44.

49. Thompson, 'What's So New about New Municipalism?'.

50. Bookchin, M. 2014. *The Next Revolution: Popular Assemblies and the Promise of Direct Democracy.* Verso.

51. Harvey, D. 2012. *Rebel Cities: From the Right to the City to the Urban Revolution.* Verso; Kolioulis, A. and Süß, R.S. (eds) 2018. 'Radical Cities: Rebel Democracy'. *Engagée,* 6(7). Available at: https://issuu.com/engagee/docs/engage_e_6_7_issuu (accessed 20 May 2020).

52. Thompson, 'What's So New about New Municipalism?'.

53. Harvey, D. 2008. 'The Right to the City'. *New Left Review,* 53, pp. 23–40.

54. Quoted in Ordóñez, V., Feenstra, R.A. and Franks, B. 2018. 'Spanish Anarchist Engagements in Electoralism: From Street to Party Politics'. *Social Movement Studies,* 17(1), pp. 85–9.

55. Ordóñez et al., 'Spanish Anarchist Engagements', p. 89.

56. Ordóñez et al., 'Spanish Anarchist Engagements', p. 89.

57. Davis, M. 2018. *Old Gods, New Enigmas: Marx's Lost Theory.* Verso; Thompson, 'What's So New about New Municipalism?'.

58. Rubio-Pueyo, B.V. 2017. 'Municipalism in Spain: From Barcelona to Madrid, and Beyond'. Rosa Luxemburg Stiftung. Available at: www.rosalux-nyc. org/municipalism-in-spain/ (accessed 10 June 2020).

59. Colau, A. 2018. 'Barcelona no s'atura'. Available at: www.youtube.com/watch?v=PGRgv8DD3-0&t=1s (accessed June 18 2020).

60. Barcelona International Welcome. 2020. 'An Open, Successful and Cohesive City to Leave Nobody Behind'. Available at: www.barcelona. cat/internationalwelcome/en/noticia/an-open-successful-and-cohesive-city-to-leave-nobody-behind_667689 (accessed 15 December 2020).

61. Barcelona International Welcome. 2020. 'Reception, Accommodation and Care'. Available at: https://ciutatrefugi.barcelona/en/reception-accommodation-and-care (accessed June 18 2020).

Chapter 6

1. The political alliance of four central European countries (Czech Republic, Hungary, Poland and Slovakia). These countries have successfully fermented anti-refugee sentiments within the EU. When migration flows increased in 2015 Hungary closed its borders leaving thousands stranded and increasing the pressure on other European countries. See BBC News. 2015. 'Migrant Crisis: Hungary's Closed Border Leaves Many Stranded'. Available at: www.bbc.com/news/world-europe-34260071 (accessed 16 December 2020). Furthermore, the group has collectively refused to accept the EU refugee relocation quota. See Zachová, A., Zgut, E., Zbytniewska, K., Strzałkowski, M. and Gabrizova, Z. 2018. 'Visegrad Nations United against Mandatory Relocation Quotas'. Euractiv.com. Available at: www.euractiv.com/section/justice-home-affairs/news/visegrad-nations-united-against-mandatory-relocation-quotas/ (accessed 16 December 2020).

2. The 'frugal four' are a group of Northern European countries including Austria, the Netherlands, Sweden and Denmark who blocked more generous recovery funds assisting the EU member states suffering the economic effects of the pandemic while securing for themselves significant budget rebates. See, e.g., Khan, M. and Peel, M. 2020. 'Frugal Four Fight to Protect EU Budget Rebates'. *Financial Times*, 18 August. Available at: www.ft.com/content/55f6796e-4a9f-43b2-8d94-da0804d1f83b (accessed 18 August 2020).

3. García Agustín, Ó. 2020, *Left-wing Populism*: The Politics of the People, Emerald Points, p. 101; De Cleen, B. 2017 'Populism and Nationalism', in Kaltwasser, C. R., Paul Taggart,P. Paula Ochoa Espejo, P. and Pierre Ostiguy, P. *The Oxford Handbook of Populism*. Oxford University Press.

4. For this discussion see Katsambekis, G., and Stavrakakis, Y. 2017. Revisiting the nationalism/populism nexus: Lessons from the Greek case. Javnost – The Public, 24:4, pp. 391–408; García Agustín, Ó. 2020. *Left-wing Populism*: *The Politics of the People*. Emerald Points.

5. Proposed by García Agustín, *Left-wing Populism*, p. 70.

6. Catalonia regained some regional autonomy after the death of General Franco in 1975 and progressively won more judicial and taxation powers. Catalonia held a referendum for full independence in 2014 and another in October 2017. In both cases the independence side won but it was found to be unconstitutional and was not recognized by Madrid. Bitter clashes marked the referendums and the leaders were prosecuted and imprisoned.

7. Burgen, S. 2018. '"Tourists Go Home, Refugees Welcome": Why Barcelona Chose Migrants over Visitors'. *The Guardian*. Available at: www.theguardian.com/cities/2018/jun/25/tourists-go-home-refugees-welcome-why-barcelona-chose-migrants-over-visitors (accessed 16 December 2020).

8. European Parliament. 2008. 'On the Evaluation of the Dublin System'. Available at: www.europarl.europa.eu/sides/getDoc.do?reference=A6-2008-0287&type=REPORT&language=EN&redirect (accessed 16 December 2020).

9. Eurostat. 2015. 'Record Number of Over 1.2 Million First Time Asylum Seekers Registered in 2015'. Available at: https://ec.europa.eu/eurostat/web/products-press-releases/-/3-04032016-AP (accessed 16 December 2020).

10. Pew Research Center's Global Attitudes Project. 2016. 'Record 1.3 Million Sought Asylum in Europe in 2015'. Available at: www.pewresearch.org/global/2016/08/02/number-of-refugees-to-europe-surges-to-record-1-3-million-in-2015/ (accessed 16 December 2020).

11. AP News. 2015. 'Greece Grants Nationality to 2nd Generation Immigrants'. Available at: https://apnews.com/article/545738a74add4464aa018efod0a6703b (accessed 16 December 2020).

12. Featherstone, D. and Karaliotas, L. 2019. 'What Are the Possibilities – and Potential Problems – of Left Populism?' *Soundings*, 72, pp. 31–47, p. 39.

13. Prentoulis, M. and Thomassen, L. 2013, 'Political Theory in the Square: Protest, Representation and Subjectification'. *Contemporary Political Theory*, 12(3), pp. 166–84.

14. García Agustín, *Left-wing Populism*, p. 69.

15. The most prominent discussion on sovereignty behind much of these debates was the idea of 'monetary sovereignty', which according to many members of the Left Platform (Syriza's formation of the more traditional left within the party whose members defected after the signing of the memorandum and Syriza's 'honourable compromise') could not happen without a major social rupture, a rupture that Syriza's compromise prevented.

16. Connolly, W.E. 2002. *Identity/Difference*. University of Minnesota Press, p. xxvi.

17. For these debates see, among others, Burges, S.W. 2007. 'Building a Global Southern Coalition: The Competing Approaches of Brazil's Lula and Venezuela's Chávez'. *Third World Quarterly*, 28(7), pp. 1343–58; and French, J.D. 2009. 'Understanding the Politics of Latin America's Plural Lefts (Chavez/Lula): Social Democracy, Populism and Convergence on the Path to a Post-neoliberal World'. *Third World Quarterly*, 30(2), pp. 349–69.

18. The discussion on Latin American populism is based on an earlier publication: Prentoulis, M. 2016. 'From the EU to Latin America: Left

Populism and Regional Integration'. *Soundings: A Journal of Politics and Culture*, 63: Spaces of Resistance, Summer, pp. 25–37.

19. This was changed to the Bolivarian Alliance for the Peoples of Our Americas in the 2009 summit to signify that the FTAA was no longer a threat.

20. Petrocaribe was set up in 2005 as an oil alliance between 18 countries of Central America and the Caribbean. CELAC (Community of Latin American and Caribbean States) was set up in 2011 with 33 Latin American and Caribbean member states. UNASUR is an economic and political alliance of twelve South American states, set up after a meeting in 2004.

21. Press Office. 2015. 'Interview of the Prime Minister to ERT1'. 15 July.

22. Prentoulis, M. 2018. 'Greece May Still Be Europe's Sick Patient, but the EU Is at Death's Door'. *The Guardian*. Available at: www.theguardian. com/commentisfree/2018/aug/21/greece-europe-eu-austerity (accessed 21 August 2018).

23. Press Office, 'Interview of the Prime Minister to ERT1'.

24. Press Office. 2017. 'Two Years of a Left Government'. 24 January.

25. Mudde, C. 2015. 'After Syriza's Landslide: Five Predictions of a Much Similar Future'. *Open Democracy*. Available at: www.opendemocracy. net/en/can-europe-make-it/after-syrizas-landslide-five-predictions-of-much-similar-future/ (accessed 16 December 2020).

26. See Anderson, B. 1991. *Imagined Communities: Reflections on the Origin and Spread of Nationalism*, revised and extended ed. Verso.

27. Larsen, H. 1999. 'British and Danish European Policies in the 1990s: A Discourse Approach'. *European Journal of International Relations*, 5(4), pp. 451–83, p. 459.

28. Diez, T. 2001. 'Europe as a Discursive Battleground: Discourse Analysis and European Integration Studies'. *Cooperation and Conflict*, 36(1), pp. 5–38.

29. Willetts, D. 1992. *Modern Conservatism*. Penguin.

30. Diez, T. 2001. 'Europe as a Discursive Battleground: Discourse Analysis and European Integration Studies'. *Cooperation and Conflict*, 36(1), pp. 5–38, p. 23.

31. BBC News. 2019. 'Supreme Court: Suspending Parliament Was Unlawful, Judges Rule'. Available at: www.bbc.com/news/uk-politics-49810261 (accessed 16 December 2020).

32. Espinoza, J. et al. 2020. 'Apple Wins Landmark Court Battle with EU over 14.3bn of tax payments'. *Financial Times*. Available at: www.ft.com/content/1c38fdc1-c4b3-4835-919d-df51698f18c4 (accessed July 17 2020).

33. Taxation and Customs Union – European Commission. 2013. 'Taxation of the Financial Sector – Taxation and Customs Union – European Commission'. Available at: https://ec.europa.eu/taxation_customs/taxation-financial-sector_en (accessed 16 December 2020).

34. Piketty, T. 2014. 'Our Manifesto for Europe'. *The Guardian*. Available at: www.theguardian.com/commentisfree/2014/may/02/manifesto-europe-radical-financial-democratic (accessed 16 December 2020).

35. Dearden, N. 2020. *Trade Secrets: The Truth about the US Trade Deal and How We Can Stop It*. Global Justice Now, p. 73.

36. Diez, T. 2001. 'Europe as a Discursive Battleground: Discourse Analysis and European Integration Studies'. *Cooperation and Conflict*, 36(1), pp. 5–38, p. 28.

37. The discussion on Brexit has been covered in a series of the author's articles in a number of left and centre-left Greek newspapers (*Avgi, Epoxi* and *Ef.Syn*) between 2016 and 2020.

38. Labour Party. 2017. 'Teresa May's Failed Brexit Plan. Available at: https://labour.org.uk/wp-content/uploads/2018/09/Theresa-Mays-failed-Brexit-plan-STRICTLY-EMBARGOED-UNTIL-2230-Monday-24-September.pdf (accessed 15 August 2020).

39. Pickard, J. 2020. 'Why Keir Starmer Wants Brexit Done'. *Financial Times*, September 16. Available at: www.ft.com/content/e3e26a2d-76c7-4fbb-beba-9baf77733f96 (accessed 16 September 2020).

40. Chrysopoulos, P. 2018. 'French Party Leader Wants SYRIZA Out of European Left'. *Greek Reporter*. Available at: https://greece.greekreporter.com/2018/02/01/french-party-leader-wants-syriza-out-of-european-left/ (accessed 20 August 2020).

41. Laireche, R. 2018. 'Immigration: Jean-Luc Mélenchon tente de dissiper les ambiguïtés'. *Liberation*. Available at: www.liberation.fr/france/2018/09/09/immigration-jean-luc-melenchon-tente-de-dissiper-les-ambiguites_1677612 (accessed 16 December 2020).

42. Varoufakis, Y. 2019. 'My First Speech as Mera25 Leader in Parliament: With English Subtitles'. Available at: www.yanisvaroufakis.eu/2019/08/06/my-first-speech-as-mera25-leaderin-parliament-with-english-subtitles (accessed 14 January 2021).

43. Fanouris, E. and Guerra, S. 2020. 'Veridiction and Leadership in Transnational Populism: The Case of DiEM25'. *Politics and Governance*, 8(1), pp. 217–25.

44. García Agustín, *Left-wing Populism*, p. 111.

Conclusion

1. It is also called the 'third economic adjustment program' or the 'third bailout package', which set the rules for financial assistance from the Troika to Greece. This lending agreement demanded structural adjustments of the Greek economy, such as privatizations and changes in the labour law, and imposed severe austerity. The country accumulated a huge debt which in 2015 had reached 175 per cent of GDP (mainly owned by financial institutions), and despite calls for it to be written off

this never materialized. Today the Greek debt is at similar heights but is considered 'sustainable', with repayments due to continue until the 2060s. Meanwhile the economy is not forecast to return to its pre-crisis size until 2030s. Wolf, M. 2019. 'Greek Economy Shows Promising Signs of Growth'. *Financial Times*. Available at: www.ft.com/content/b42ee1ac-4a27-11e9-bde6-79eaea5acb64 (accessed 14 January 2021).

2. Naftemporiki. 2020. 'Αλ. Τσίπρας: Μας φοβούνται γιατί κατάλαβαν πως δεν θα τους επιτρέψουμε να περάσουν τα σχέδιά τους'. Available at: https://m.naftemporiki.gr/story/1616878/al-tsipras-mas-fobountai-giati-katalaban-pos-den-tha-tous-epitrepsoume-na-perasoun-ta-sxedia-tous (accessed 16 December 2020).

3. The Press Project. 2020. '*Λιγότερο Από Το* 1% *Στον Αντιπολιτευόμενο Τύπο Για Το «Μένουμε Σπίτι*'. Available at: https://thepressproject.gr/ligotero-apo-to-1-ston-antipolitevomeno-typo-gia-to-menoume-spiti/?fbclid=IwAR0iX7ANNNy5iqarfBIhhyNWLgj9q1Qiz_xYNGquk123P7PhSfBtYVg2PlA (accessed 16 December 2020).

4. Αυγή. 2020. 'Λίστα Πέτσα / Δεκάδες χιλιάδες ευρώ σε κανάλι αρνητών μάσκας και συνωμοσιολόγων'. Available at: www.avgi.gr/koinonia/368237_dekades-hiliades-eyro-se-kanali-arniton-maskas-kai-synomosiologon (accessed 16 December 2020).

5. Bellos, I. 2020. 'Tourism Income Seen 80% Off'. *Ekathimerini*, 22 August. Available at: www.ekathimerini.com/256076/article/ekathimerini/business/tourism-income-seen-80-off (accessed 4 October 2020).

6. TVXS – TV Χωρίς Σύνορα. 2020. 'Η Κυβέρνηση Δίνει Διπλάσια Αποζημίωση Σε Ιδιωτικές Κλινικές Για Κρεβάτια ΜΕΘ'. Available at: https://tvxs.gr/news/ellada/i-kybernisi-dinei-diplasia-apozimiosi-se-idiotikes-klinikes-gia-krebatia-meth (accessed 16 December 2020).

7. Interview, Vasilis Skouras with Alexis Tsipras. Σκουρής, Β. 2020. '*Αλέξης Τσίπρας Στο* Ieidiseis: Απέτυχε Σε Όλα Τα Μέτωπα Ο Μητσοτάκης - Διεκδικούμε Πλειοψηφία Για Να Βγάλουμε Τη Χώρα Από Το Τέλμα'. Ieidiseis.gr. Available at: www.ieidiseis.gr/politiki/item/55192-aleksis-tsipras-sto-ieidiseis-apetyxe-se-ola-ta-metopa-o-mitsotakis-diekdikoyme-pleiopsifia-gia-na-vgaloume-ti-xora-apo-to-telma (accessed 16 December 2020).

8. Interview, Vasilis Skouras with Alexis Tsipras. Σκουρής, '*Αλέξης Τσίπρας Στο* Ieidiseis'.

9. One of these cases was the raiding of a popular club where the police asked 300 revellers to kneel on the floor with their hands behind their heads for hours. The police justification of drug dealing in the place collapsed when only insignificant quantities of drugs were found.

10. See Barlett, N. 2020. 'Momentum Sends Members a Labour Leadership Ballot with Rebecca Long-Bailey as the Only Option'. Available at: www.mirror.co.uk/news/politics/backlash-after-momentum-sends-members-21283993 (accessed 16 December 2020).

11. See Rodgers, S. 2020. 'Victory for Forward Momentum Candidates As Lansman Steps Down'. *LabourList*. Available at: https://labourlist.org/2020/07/victory-for-forward-momentum-candidates-as-lansman-steps-down/ (accessed 16 December 2020).

12. Telesurenglish.net. 2020. 'Spain's Government Raises Taxes to Large Fortunes and Companies'. Available at: www.telesurenglish.net/news/Spains-Government-Raises-Taxes-To-Large-Fortunes-and-Companies-20201027-0010.html (accessed 16 December 2020).

13. Interview, Vasilis Skouras with Alexis Tsipras. Σκουρής, 'Αλέξης Τσίπρας Στο Ieidiseis'.

Index

Note: EU refers to European Union; GFC refers to the Global Financial Crisis (2008)